A Passion for
HORSES

A Passion for
HORSES

Caroline Lemay

METRO BOOKS
New York

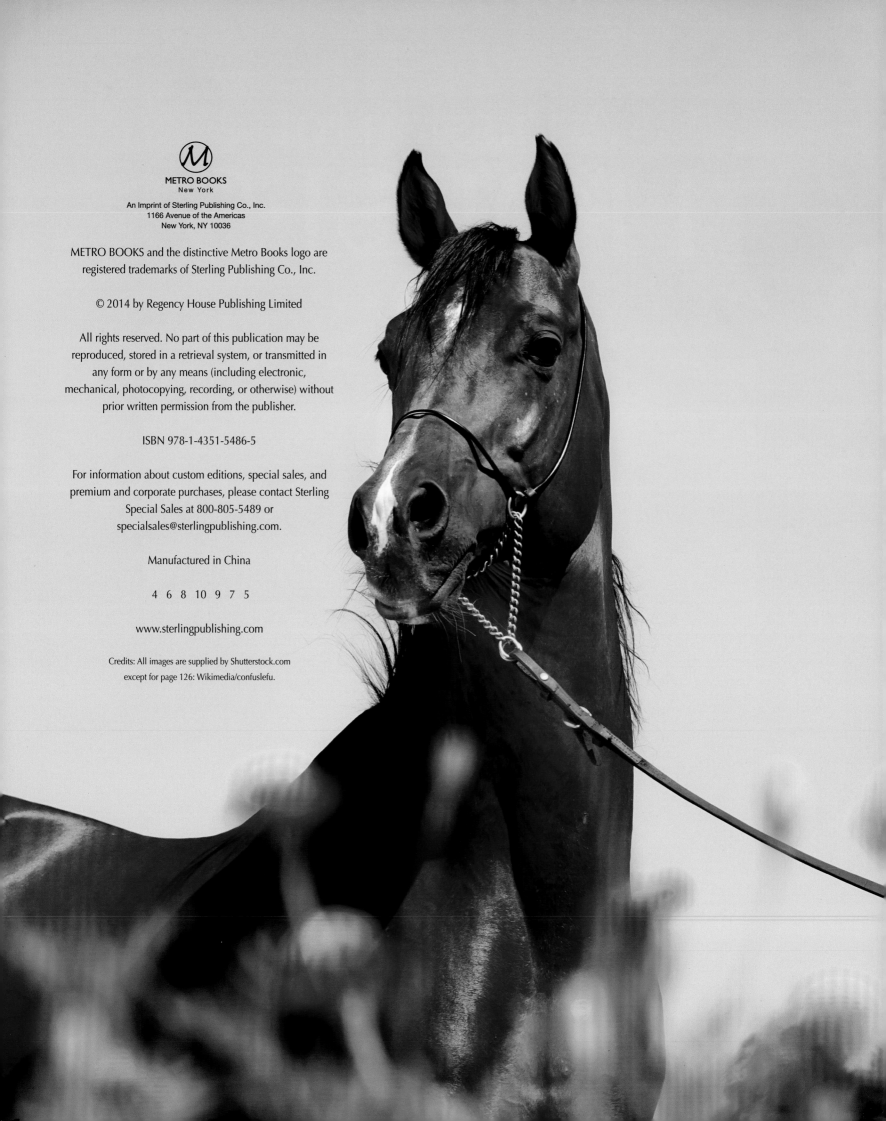

METRO BOOKS
New York

An Imprint of Sterling Publishing Co., Inc.
1166 Avenue of the Americas
New York, NY 10036

ISBN 978-1-4351-5486-5

For information about custom editions, special sales, and premium and corporate purchases, please contact Sterling Special Sales at 800-805-5489 or specialsales@sterlingpublishing.com.

Manufactured in China

4 6 8 10 9 7 5

www.sterlingpublishing.com

Credits: All images are supplied by Shutterstock.com except for page 126: Wikimedia/confuslefu.

CONTENTS

INTRODUCTION
6

Chapter One
WILD HORSES
8

Chapter Two
HORSES OF THE AMERICAS
32

Chapter Three
HORSES OF WESTERN EUROPE
76

Chapter Four
HORSES OF EASTERN EUROPE
184

Chapter Five
HORSES OF ASIA
206

Chapter Six
HORSES OF AUSTRALIA & AFRICA
224

Chapter Six
HEAVY HORSES
234

INDEX
254

A PASSION FOR HORSES
Caroline Lemay

I have been enchanted with horses for as long as I can remember. I was attracted rather than intimidated by their great size and as a tiny child wanted nothing more than to be with them, to smell their sweet breath, to hear their neighs and the sound of their hooves resonating on the ground. Many would think that loving horses is all about riding them, but to me it is the entire relationship, built up over the years, that is the most rewarding part.

When I first joined the local riding school, I knew that learning to ride horses was not going to be enough for me, so I became involved with their mucking out, grooming and other duties around the stable yard – I just couldn't keep away – which was enough to persuade my parents that this was no short-lived craze. They bought me a pony of my own, which was like being in heaven and was when I discovered the meaning of true happiness! As I gained more and more knowledge of the equestrian world, it was not long before I was breaking, schooling and competing horses. I was hooked for life!

But it must not be forgotten that horses are spirited, high-strung creatures, so managing them is not always plain sailing; domesticated horses retain elements of behavior, inherited from their wild ancestors that demand tact and sympathy from their handlers, for despite being outwardly powerful and immensely strong there is a sensitive side to their nature which must not go unregarded. This is the great paradox that makes the relationship between horse and handler all the more fascinating, despite needing work and commitment to achieve that may even involve a few sleepless nights.

Eventually, however, there comes a time when the hard work seems to pay off, and there is that euphoric moment when horse and rider achieve perfect rapport. But remember that horses cannot be forced to do anything they do not really want to do: I remember many a time trying to catch a horse that has decided the exact opposite and nothing in the world is going to make him budge, or the time when, inexplicably and unpredictably, he decides to cast his rider from his back!

But to me, the great beauty of the horse is the way that it combines athleticism with incomparable grace and nobility of spirit. You will discover that your horse will want to please you once mutual trust and a true and lasting bond has been forged.

CHAPTER ONE
WILD HORSES

"...I heard a neigh. Oh, such a brisk and melodious neigh as that was!
My very heart leaped with delight at the sound."

—Nathaniel Hawthorne

Mankind's encounters with horses, throughout much of history, have been with the domesticated kind, for the horse has lived side by side with us for thousands of years. Once used as warhorses, as beasts of burden and for transporting human beings, the horse's modern-day purpose seems to be solely for our pleasure, all of which are a far cry from its true evolution as a wild, free-roaming herd animal.

Naturally gregarious and highly social, horses are at their happiest with others of their kind, surrounded by plenty of open space, so it is hardly surprising that once freedom is allowed they should revert to natural behavior. In the wild, horses form themselves into a herd, with a dominant stallion as their leader, which protects its group of mares and youngsters. The herd forms a close unit, its

members playing, grooming, feeding and resting together, all the while keeping a watchful eye for signs of danger. During the mating season, the stallion will fight for herd dominance, securing for itself plenty of breeding females in the process.

Horses have evolved to be perfectly adapted to living in the open. They are powerful sprinters capable of achieving significant speeds when fleeing from danger. They have large eyes, set on the sides of their heads, which provide almost all-round vision. They also have extremely good hearing, and their mobile, pointed ears allow them to catch sounds from all angles.

The instinct to herd provides the group with relative safety compared with that of a lone animal; a galloping group tends to confuse would-be predators, while any animal that is brought down would more likely be one that is weak or sick.

The term "wild horse" is also used colloquially to refer to free-roaming herds of feral horses such as the Mustang in the United States, the Brumby in Australia, and many others. These feral horses are untamed members of the domestic horse subspecies (*Equus ferus caballus*) and should not be confused with the two truly "wild" horse subspecies, the Tarpan or Eurasian Wild Horse (*Equus ferus ferus*), once native to Europe and western Asia, and Przewalski's Horse (*Equus ferus przewalskii*).

OPPOSITE: A herd of wild German Dülmen ponies at a gallop.

ABOVE: Wild horses in the Torres del Paine National Park, Patagonia, Chile.

RIGHT: Two wild Mustangs.

BRUMBY

Australia had no native horses of its own until they were introduced during the country's gradual colonization, and in particular by settlers, who arrived during the 19th-century gold rush. Not only was there an influx of people, therefore, but also a large intake of horses and other animals.

During the First World War, many of the horses escaped or were turned loose to run wild: these were the forefathers of the modern-day Brumby, a name said to have been derived from the aboriginal word for "wild" (*baroomby*).

Because of the variety of animals that reverted to a wild state, there is no specific breed type; consequently Brumbies come in all shapes, sizes and colors.

The horses are now almost totally feral, making them difficult to catch and almost impossible to train. They are prolific breeders and for this reason, in the past, have come to be regarded as pests. This has led to such extensive culling that they are now quite rare. They come in all colors and patterns. Height is up to 15hh.

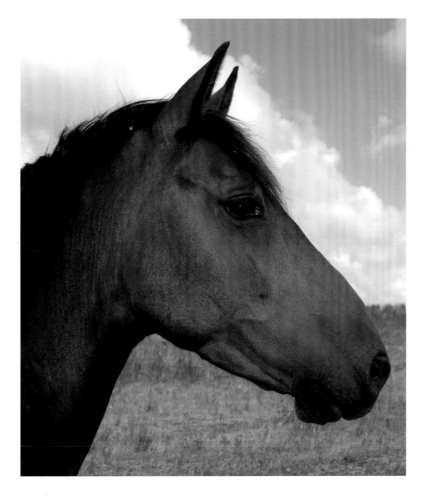

THESE PAGES & OVERLEAF: Reminiscent of the American Mustang, Brumbies are the largest group of horses in the world that live in a wild state.

CAMARGUE

The salt marshes and lagoons of the Rhône delta, located south of Arles in France, are home to a race of semi-wild horses that spend their time grazing the sparse vegetation. This is a very ancient breed that bears a striking resemblance to the primitive horses painted on cave-walls at Lascaux in prehistoric times. The Camargue's qualities were appreciated by Roman invaders on their way to the Iberian Peninsula, with the result that connections were inevitably made with Spanish breeds.

The breed was further enhanced in the 19th century by infusions of Postier Breton, Arab, Thoroughbred and Anglo-Arab

ABOVE & RIGHT: It would be unthinkable to visit the Camargue without seeing the famous white horses that have been roaming there for centuries.

bloodlines, though they seem to have had little bearing on the horses' overall appearance.

There is a round-up in the Camargue every year, when suitable horses are selected for riding purposes and substandard animals are culled: this may seem ruthless but there is no doubt that it has led to improvements in the breed.

Camargue horses are traditionally ridden by the *gardiens* (Camargue cowboys), who use them for herding the famous black bulls of the region and for festivals in which their dazzling feats of horsemanship are displayed. The horses are also used for trekking the region, now a popular tourist attraction.

The head of the Camargue (Camaguais) is rather square, with a broad forehead, short, broad ears, and expressive eyes. The neck is short and well-developed, the shoulder upright, and the back is short with a low-set tail. The legs are strong and the hooves well-shaped and tough. The mane and tail are particularly abundant.

Camargues make obedient riding horses; they are extremely agile and have the ability to turn sharply at full gallop. As trekking ponies they are sure-footed and have plenty of stamina. They never quite lose their independent spirit, however, and something of their wild inheritance is always retained. They are invariably white (gray), though other colors sometimes appear. Foals are born dark but their coats grow lighter as they mature. Height is from 13.1–14.2hh.

LEFT & ABOVE: The horses of the Camargue bear a strong resemblance to those depicted by prehistoric man on the walls of the caves at Lascaux.

KONIK

The Konik, or "little horse," resembles the wild Tarpan of eastern Europe and western Asia which is now extinct. The Konik itself is not a specific breed and there is no particular standard, but there are around five types, some with native blood and others with added Arab bloodlines.

The Konik, being related to the Tarpan, which was a small horse of Oriental origin, has a small, neat head, dorsal stripe and zebra markings. Sadly, the last remaining Tarpan died in captivity in 1887, having been hunted to extinction some ten years earlier.

In the last century, efforts were made to revive the ancient breed by preserving the Konik's Tarpan genes. These reconstituted

Tarpans, as they are now known, live wild in a nature reserve where they are beginning to manifest many Tarpan characteristics. Today Koniks are mainly used for farm work and occasionally as children's ponies.

The Konik has strong head with great character that shows its Oriental origins. The neck is of medium length and quite thick

BELOW & OVERLEAF: The Konik is the closest relative of the now-extinct Tarpan and attempts are being made to preserve the Tarpan gene pool present in the breed.

but with a good carriage. The body is stout and sturdy with well-developed, medium-length legs, which are slightly feathered. The hooves are tough.

The Konik is hardy and will live out all year round with little extra feeding and care. Some can be wilful and difficult – a throwback to their wild Tarpan origins. Usually light-brown or dun and sometimes bay, the mane and tail are full and the dorsal stripe and zebra markings are sometimes visible. Height is 12.2–13.3hh.

MUSTANG

Although horses had once been present in North America, by the time the conquistadors arrived in the Americas in the 16th century, the indigenous prehistoric horses had long been extinct. The Spanish brought Iberian horses with them in their ships, derived mainly from Arabs and Barbs. Many of these sleek, desert-bred and resilient horses were allowed to wander off, spreading into North America and forming feral rather than wild herds. They became known as Mustangs.

Native American tribes came to value the Mustang's qualities and many were caught and domesticated by them. They even

BELOW & OPPOSITE: Today, Mustangs are shadows of their former selves, but efforts are now being made to protect the breed.

developed their own breeds based on the Mustang, such as the Appaloosa, the Cayuse Indian Pony and the Chickasaw Indian Pony, also known as the Florida Cracker Horse.

There were between one- and two-million Mustangs in existence by the beginning of the 19th century, many of them still running free, though others had been caught and were being used by settlers. Unfortunately, the wild horses came to be regarded as pests, and were culled in their thousands to make way for cattle. It was not only the ranchers who were responsible for their decimation, thousands were also killed in the 20th century, sacrificed to the pet-food industry.

Sadly, there are fewer than 50,000 Mustangs in existence today, and in some areas numbers are dangerously low. Determined efforts are now being made to safeguard the breed for the future and, fortunately for the Mustang, the breed is now seen as an important part of the American heritage and a protected species.

Mustangs come in all colors, sizes and builds, although horses that display Barb characteristics are particularly favored by breeders. The Mustang is easy to train, due to its innate

THESE PAGES & OVERLEAF: Young Mustangs are relatively easy to domesticate and make excellent riding horses.

intelligence, and it is tough and resilient. It can be any color, although it is mainly brown, chestnut, bay or dun. Height varies from 14–16hh.

PRZEWALSKI'S HORSE

This is a truly ancient breed, also known as the Mongolian or Asiatic Wild Horse. Primitive horses of this kind were hunted by man 20,000 years ago and the likenesses of similar horses can be seen in prehistoric cave paintings in Spain and France. The breed was almost certainly extinct in the wild, but recent introductions of herds has led to a new population. Genetically, it is the only true wild equine and the distant ancestor of the domestic horse.

The earliest written evidence of its existence was in the 9th century, and it was mentioned again in 1226, when a herd of wild horses are supposed to have caused Ghengis Khan, the founder of the Mongol Empire, to fall from his horse.

ABOVE & RIGHT: Cooperation between the London Zoo and Mongolian scientists has resulted in a successful reintroduction of these Przewalski horses from zoos into their natural habitat in Mongolia; and there are now several hundred in the wild.

Because of its isolation and the fierceness with which stallions protect their mares, the Mongolian horse's bloodline has remained pure and can be traced back to its primitive ancestors.

It gets its modern name from the man who brought it to the attention of the world, Colonel N. M. Przewalski, a Polish explorer who acquired the remains of a wild horse in 1881 from hunters who had discovered them in the Gobi Desert. He took them to the zoological museum in St. Petersburg, where naturalist I. S. Poliakoff examined them and decided that they belonged to a species of primitive wild horse. Following the discovery, some of the living horses were caught and kept in captivity in zoos and wildlife parks so that they would be saved from total extinction.

The captive population has increased rapidly and is carefully monitored at Prague Zoo, which holds the stud book of the breed. The horses are kept in conditions that are as natural as possible;

OPPOSITE & BELOW: Unlike other "wild" breeds, Przewalskis have never been domesticated and cannot be tamed.

some have been released back into the wild in China, Russia and Mongolia, where they are a protected species, and a successful population can also be found in France.

The Przewalski is stocky and has an erect, dark-brown mane. The head is of medium size, with a broad forehead and a straight or slightly dished nose. The wild-looking eyes are set high on the head and are rather small. The nose tapers to a narrow muzzle with small, low-set nostrils. The body is strong, with a longish, straight back, a thick, short neck, and weak quarters. The legs are short and stocky with hard, tough hooves.

Przewalskis cannot be tamed and tend to be aggressive and ferocious, especially in the presence of their young. Being extremely hardy, they need very little extra attention.

Various shades of dun, ranging from yellow to red, are possible. Przewalskis have black manes and tails and black legs, often with zebra markings, and there is a black dorsal stripe running down the back. The muzzle and the area around the eyes is a creamy-white color. They range in height from 12–14hh.

CHAPTER TWO

HORSES OF THE AMERICAS

*"I can always tell which is the front end of a horse, but beyond that,
my art is not above the ordinary."*

—Mark Twain

AMERICAN MINIATURE HORSE

This is not a pony but a scaled-down version of a horse; consequently it has all the characteristics of the larger animal. The first true miniature horses appeared in Europe in the 1600s, where they were bred as pampered pets for the nobility. Unfortunately, not all miniatures had such a good life and many were used as pit ponies in the coal mines of northern Europe, including the English Midlands. In the 1900s Lady Estella Hope continued the breeding program, and these are the lines that probably made their way to the United States.

Today the American Miniature Horse is stylish, well-proportioned and the product of nearly 400 years of selective breeding. They make excellent all-rounders, especially in

BELOW & OPPOSITE: The American Miniature has a kind and gentle nature, making it ideal as a children's riding horse.

children's riding classes such as showjumping and showing, and are also used for driving. The breed now has a closed stud book managed by the American Miniature Horse Association.

The American Miniature Horse should not exceed 34 inches (86cm) or 9hh. It should have a similar conformation to a large, fine-boned horse such as a Thoroughbred or Warmblood. The overall impression should be of well-balanced symmetry, accompanied by strength, agility and alertness; essentially, it should have all the appearance of the perfect horse in miniature.

The horse has a kind and affectionate nature. It is also gentle and placid, making it an ideal companion animal. It is excellent

for children, and inspires confidence because it is easy to mount and willing to be ridden; its small stature also makes it suitable for the less physically able. The foals are particularly attractive, ranging from 16–21 inches (41–53cm) in height. They can be all colors and achieve no more than 9hh in height.

OPPOSITE & ABOVE: Although small in stature, the American Miniature is regarded as a true horse rather than a pony.

AMERICAN SADDLEBRED

The American Saddlebred was developed from horses originally brought to America from Europe in the 1600s, and particularly from Britain and what is now the Irish Republic. They had been used for trotting and pacing, and their hardy constitutions and extravagant paces made them popular in their new home.

The Narragansett Pacer, which was developed in Rhode Island in the 17th century, is believed to have been an ancestor of these European horses, and it was the model on which all easy-gaited horses in America were based thereafter.

Now extinct, the Pacer was noted for its docility and easy motion, making long days in the saddle more comfortable for the rider in the early days of the American colonies. Narragansett mares and

BELOW & RIGHT: The American Saddlebred has a charming, biddable temperament and shows great affection towards its owners.

Thoroughbred stallions were allowed to mate, with the result that the pacing gait and all-round ability were transferred to their offspring. Eventually, they were known as the American Horse, and when combined with Morgan, Standardbred and Thoroughbred blood, produced the American Saddlebred as it is known today.

While the traditional gaits of walk, trot and canter are innate, the Saddlebred is a breed apart, having inherited the ability to add additional gaits to its repertoire. These include the slow gait or running walk, the stepping pace, and the slow rack, which is when both hooves on either side are in turn lifted almost simultaneously. This means that, at certain moments, all four hooves are off the ground, which is spectacular when combined with the horse's high-stepping action.

This high-stepping carriage is sometimes falsely encouraged by keeping the feet long and building the feet up, while in other cases, the muscles under the dock are nicked to produce an unnaturally stiff and high tail-carriage: these are illegal practices in most countries of the world. The use of the tail brace also persists. This is sometimes fitted to a stabled horse in order that a high tail-carriage can be preserved; this, however, is at the expense of the horse's comfort when it is at rest. This practice should be modified or preferably banished if true recognition is to be achieved within the broader equestrian world.

The Saddlebred has a commanding presence and subtle expression of movement. The head is small and narrow, carried high, and the alert and intelligent expression is accentuated by the horse's fine pricked ears. The eyes are gentle but intelligent and the nose is straight with slightly flared nostrils. The neck is long and elegant and also carried high. The withers are high and run neatly into the back, which is fairly long, as is the barrel-shaped body. The shoulders are narrower at the top than the bottom and slope to create the trademark fluid action. The tail-carriage is naturally high, joined to flat quarters flowing into strong and powerful loins.

The Saddlebred is biddable and easy to train. It is gentle and affectionate, loves people, and enjoys being handled. At the same time, it is spirited and proud, with a keen intelligence and an alert demeanor. It tends to become excitable under saddle.

Saddlebreds come in all the usual solid colors, including palomino and roan, and there is often a good deal of white on the head and legs. The coat, mane and tail are fine and silky in texture. The horses typically range in size from 15–16.1hh.

Saddlebreds are highly prized within the show ring, particularly in the harness and riding classes in which they excel; but they are also capable of competing in other events, performing equally well as dressage horses and showjumpers.

RIGHT: The American Saddlebred is capable not only of performing the usual gaits, but also of learning additional ones, such as the slow-stepping gait and the rack.

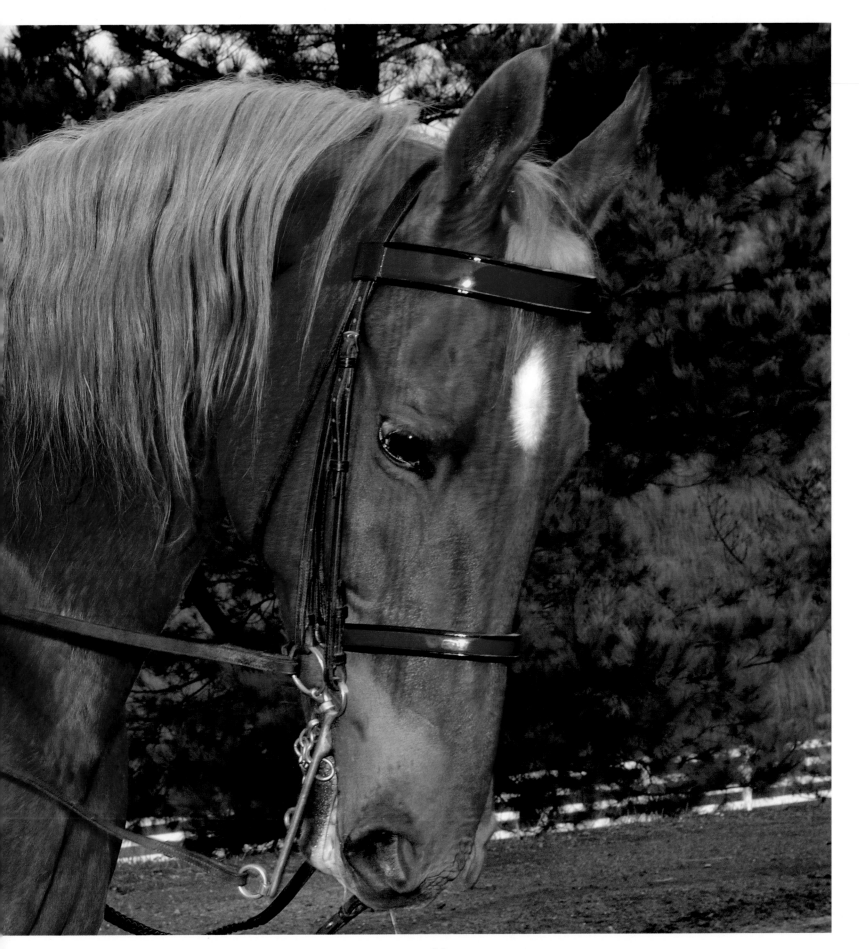

AMERICAN SHETLAND

As the name suggests, the American Shetland's ancestors were the native ponies of the Shetland Islands, situated off the northern coast of Scotland. In 1885, 75 ponies were imported to America by Eli Elliot, and were raised in the south-eastern states, where they thrived in spite of the warm, humid conditions. Their success led to the formation of the American Shetland Pony Club in 1888.

Today, the American Shetland is very different from its Scottish ancestor, being lighter in stature with longer, finer legs. This was achieved by crossing original Shetlands with small Arab, Thoroughbred and Hackney breeds, resulting in a small horse rather than a stock pony.

The American Shetland now excels in various driven classes, such as the two-wheeled roadster, four-wheeled buggy, and light sulky. It is also good with children and will happily compete in pony as well as breed classes and hunter-pony events. It is ridden in either English or Western tack.

It possesses all the showy attributes of its small horse ancestors, combined with the strength and workmanlike character of the Scottish original. The head is longish, nearer to that of a horse than a pony; the nose is straight, the ears fairly long, and the eyes are also more like those of a horse. It has retained many of the original Shetland's characteristics, in that mane and high-set tail are furnished with thick, strong hair. The neck is quite short but the legs could be considered overlong, though they have retained their strength. The hooves retain the original Shetland strength and shape.

Having many of the attributes of the horse now in its make-up, the American Shetland has an equable temperament, and its small size makes it ideal for children to ride. It is reasonably hardy, making it easy to maintain.

American Shetlands come in all the usual solid colors, including roan, dun and cream. They sometimes achieve heights in the region of 11.2hh.

BELOW & OPPOSITE: A well-trained American Shetland not only excels at driving, but its classic maximum height of only 46 inches (117cm) also makes it an excellent starter pony for a young child.

APPALOOSA

The gene that produces the many permutations of spots in horses is an ancient one, as indicated in Cro-Magnon depictions of such horses in cave paintings. For many centuries, spotted horses were highly prized in Europe and Asia and they were often featured in Chinese art. The Spanish conquistadors brought their own such horses with them on their travels, introducing the spotted gene to the Americas when they arrived. After a time, some of these horses passed to Native Americans, in particular the Nez Percé, who lived in north-eastern Oregon along the Palouse river. The Nez Percé, probably the first to introduce selective breeding, followed strict guidelines to produce the best results. They called this meeting of European and native stock the Appaloosa – possibly America's oldest breed.

Settlers eventually eliminated the Nez Percé, and the Appaloosa was dispersed throughout the land, the strain becoming weakened through random breeding. Nowadays the Appaloosa is enjoying renewed popularity. It does not have to be spotted, however, although it is mandatory that other criteria be present: the Appaloosa must have sclera around the eyeballs, striped hooves, and mottled skin beneath the hair.

The Appaloosa is a most versatile horse and looks good wearing Western tack. It is commonly used in Western events, such as roping, working cowhorse, and barrel-racing competitions. It is also used for showing, particularly in Britain, in riding horse and colored horse classes, and is proficient at cross-country and jumping.

There are some obvious differences between American and European Appaloosas. The U.S. types have been crossed with Quarter Horses, with the result that their size and conformation are similar. In Europe, Appaloosas are rather larger, nearer to the size of a warmblood, making them ideal for jumping and dressage purposes. The type is also becoming popular in the United States.

After the formation of the Appaloosa Horse Club in 1938, a more modern type developed with the addition of Arabian bloodlines, while the Quarter Horse element produced Appaloosas that performed better in sprint racing and in halter competition. In fact, many cutting and reining horses resulted from old-type Appaloosas crossed on Arabian bloodlines.

An infusion of Thoroughbred blood was added during the 1970s to produce horses more suited for racing. Many current breeders also attempt to breed away from the sparse, 'rat tail' trait, with the result that modern Appaloosas have fuller manes and tails.

The Appaloosa is a workmanlike horse, with a fairly plain head and short, tapered ears. The eyes are alert and inquisitive, with the mandatory white rings or sclera around the eyeball rims. The neck and body are compact and well-muscled and the quarters are powerful with well-developed limbs. The tail and mane hair is relatively sparse. Hooves should be striped.

Appaloosas are great all-rounders: they are good-natured and hardy with plenty of stamina, speed and agility.

Color patterns include Blanket, which is a solid white area, normally over the quarters and loins, with a contrasting base color; Spots, when white or dark spots cover all or a portion of the body; Blanket with Spots, when there is a white blanket with dark spots within the white area, usually in the same color as the base color; Roan, when a lighter-colored area develops on the face and over the back, loins and quarters; Roan Blanket with Spots, when there is a roan blanket which has white and/or dark spots within the roan area; Solid, when a base color has no contrasting color in the form of an Appaloosa coat pattern. Appaloosas usually attain a height of between 14.2 and 15.2hh.

THESE PAGES & OVERLEAF: The Appaloosa is regarded as the archetypal American horse. Developed from European and American bloodlines, it has gained popularity as a versatile riding horse.

CRIOLLO

The Spanish conquistadors brought the horse to the Americas and they could have done nothing better than to introduce the Arab, Barb and excellent Iberian. It is these three bloodlines that went into the making of the Criollo, the native horse of Argentina. For many hundreds of years the Criollo roamed the treeless plains (pampas) of Argentina, where pitiless natural selection helped to form it into one of the toughest horses in the world.

Criollos eventually came to be ridden by gauchos, or South American cowboys, who also used them as packhorses, having been quick to recognize their excellent hardiness, stamina, speed and resilience.

The Criollo is tough, can survive on next to nothing, and is an obedient worker. It is able to withstand some of the harshest conditions in the world.

Today, herds live in a semi-wild condition on the enormous ranches of South America, where they are caught and broken in as required. They are still used as stock and riding horses, and they make excellent polo ponies when crossed with Thoroughbreds.

Rigorous endurance tests to evaluate Criollos for breeding are used where horses ride over a 466-mile (750-km) course, carrying a load of 245lb (111kg), to be completed in a set time. During this time, the horses feed only on what they can forage for themselves, and they are checked by veterinarians once the test has been completed.

The Criollo's toughness is more than obvious from its stocky exterior. The head is broad with wide-set eyes and the nose is slightly dished. It has fairly large ears. The neck is well-developed with a wide back and chest and strong quarters. The back is also short, with sloping shoulders, and the short, sturdy legs possess plenty of bone.

Color is most commonly dun, with a black mane and tail, an eel stripe down the center of the back, and zebra markings on the legs. Other colors are chestnut, bay, black, roan, gray, piebald, skewbald and palomino. Height is from 14–15hh.

LEFT: These days, the Criollo is becoming something of a rarity, although steps are being taken to protect the breed.

FALABELLA

It is said that the Falabella's ancestors were first seen in the 19th century, interspersed with the herds of South American Indians. But it was more probably the creation of the Falabella family, at their ranch near Buenos Aires in Argentina, over a century ago. The breed was established by first crossing small Arab and Thoroughbred stallions with Shetland Pony mares. Then, using selective breeding, it was made ever smaller.

The Falabella is not a pony: it is a miniature horse with all the conformation and character of a horse. Because of excessive in-breeding, however, the conformation of some individuals is far from ideal, consequently they tend to look rather odd. They are also weak

THESE PAGES & OVERLEAF: The tiny Falabella is not classified as a pony but as a small horse, although one that is capable of being ridden only by very small children.

for their size and can be ridden only by the smallest children. Today, breeders are attempting to rectify these faults and are generally trying to improve the breed.

Being affectionate, Falabellas make ideal pets and are sometimes allowed even into peoples' homes because of their small size. They are popular in special in-hand showing classes and are capable of pulling small carts.

Correctly bred, a Fallabella should resemble a miniature Thoroughbred or Arab, though its Shetland ancestry may occasionally come to the fore. The head is refined and horse-like, with a straight nose and small, flared nostrils. The small ears are set wide apart, and the eyes are kind. The body is medium-length, with a slim frame, and the legs are fine, similar to those of a Thoroughbred.

The Falabella is a delightful breed. It provides all the pleasures of a larger breed but at a lower cost; this is particularly true as far as land requirements are concerned. Its constitution, however, is less that robust and it requires the same care that one would give to any finely bred horse. It is amenable, docile and obedient.

Falabellas come in all solid colors, as well as gray and roan, and Appaloosa markings are also common. Ideally, they should stand no taller than 30in (76cm) from the ground.

MANGALARGA MARCHADOR

Brazil and Portugal have been closely connected for centuries, and at one time even had the same ruler, Don João VI, in around 1815. It was he who was responsible for bringing quality Portuguese and Spanish horses to Brazil, particularly the Andalusian and the Altér Real.

The Brazilian Mangalarga is a direct descendant of one particular Altér Real stallion, which was mated with Criollo mares, though more Altér Real, Barb and Andalusian were eventually added to improve the breed. The result is neat, lightly built, and strongly reminiscent of the Barb but with the rolling gait of the Spanish breeds.

The Mangalarga is most often used on the enormous estancias of Brazil, where its fifth gait, known as the *marcha*, makes it fast but comfortable to ride. It has a smooth, stable walk, canter and gallop, as well as a natural diagonal (*batida*) or lateral (*picada*) four-beat gait.

The Mangalarga's head is high and proud, with medium-length ears, intelligent eyes, and a nose that is straight with flaring nostrils. The back is long with strong loins and neat quarters; the shoulders are sloping with a deep girth, and there are well-muscled legs with hard hooves.

The Mangalarga has incredible stamina, and this enables it to work all day and cover huge distances. It is good-natured, willing and obedient. Coat colors are usually bay, gray, chestnut and roan. Height is around 15hh.

OPPOSITE & BELOW: Today, the Mangalarga Marchador is used for endurance and trail-riding, jumping and polo. It is an excellent and versatile riding and showing horse.

MISSOURI FOX TROTTER

The Missouri Fox Trotter was developed in the 19th century by settlers in Missouri and Arkansas. Initially, its purpose was to be a general riding horse, with the speed and endurance to cope with difficult terrain. The foundation stock for the breed was the Morgan, which was infused with Thoroughbred and Arab as well as Iberian blood.

As horses with elaborate gaits became more popular, the breed was later mated with the Saddlebred and Tennessee Walking Horse, which greatly improved its elegance, bearing and paces, including

BELOW & RIGHT: The Missouri Fox Trotter is named for its extra foxtrot gait, in which it appears to be walking with the front legs while trotting with the hind.

its foxtrot gait; this is basically a diagonal gait, like the trot, in which the horse appears to be walking with the front legs while trotting with the hind.

In the early days, the Fox Trotter had been a useful competitor in racing, but increasingly has reverted to its use as a general riding horse.

A stud book for the breed was eventually opened in 1948. The breed society, however, put in place strict guidelines that the

Missouri Fox Trotter should have no artificial aids to influence and enhance its gait, such as nicking or setting the tail; consequently its action is not as pronounced or extravagant as that of the American Saddlebred, for example. The breed is popular in the United States, where it is used for general riding, showing and endurance.

The head is a little plain, with a straight nose and a square muzzle with large open nostrils. The ears are medium-length and alert and the eyes have a kind but intelligent expression. The neck is medium-length and fairly well-developed, with prominent withers; the back is short, with strong loins and hindquarters. The tail is set fairly low, and the legs are long with large joints and well-shaped, strong hooves.

The Missouri Fox Trotter has a charming, easy-going manner. It is willing and obedient with excellent stamina and endurance. It comes in colors and can also be part-colored. Height is from 14–16hh.

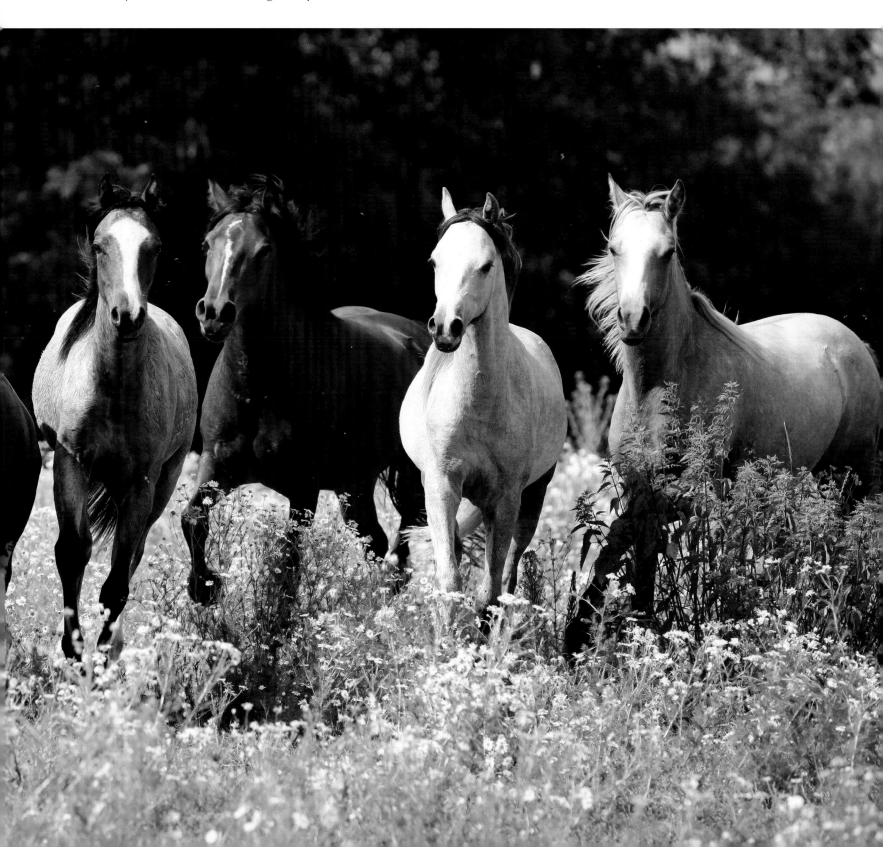

MORGAN

One of America's most famous and versatile breeds, all Morgans can be traced back to just one stallion called Figure. Figure was later renamed Justin Morgan after its owner, Thomas Justin Morgan, a tavern keeper and singing teacher, who supplemented his income by breeding stallions.

The colt was born in around 1790 in Vermont. It is thought that its sire was probably a Welsh Cob, called True Briton, though little is known of the dam, other than that she may have had Oriental and Thoroughbred blood.

Thomas Justin Morgan was so impressed with his stallion's looks and personality that he eventually decided to put him to stud. The results were remarkable in that a foal the image of its father was always produced no matter what mare Justin Morgan covered. The sire's prowess as a marvellous harness and riding horse, moreover,

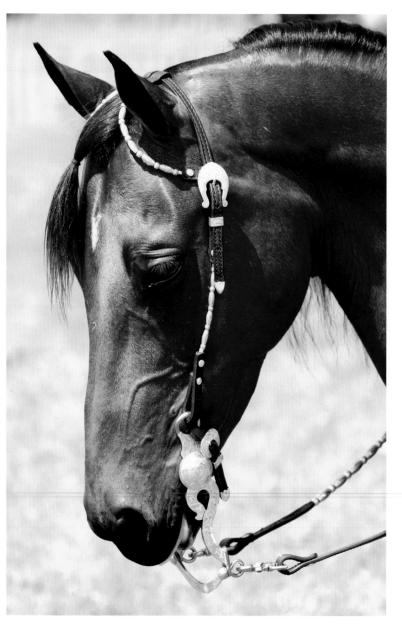

seemed to be replicated in the offspring, the performance of each of them being second to none. In fact, all were amazed that such a significant and impressive breed could have developed from a single stallion.

Morgans are just as versatile today – used in harness competitions, shows, driving and trail-riding. They are strong and hard-working, and have a spirited but tractable nature.

The head should provide immediate evidence of quality, with beautiful and expressive eyes. The muzzle is small and the profile straight or slightly dished. The neck is well-crested and the shoulders strong. The hindquarters are large and strong and the legs sturdy.

A type known as the Park Morgan is bred particularly for its high-stepping action. Another type is the Pleasure Morgan, whose action is less exaggerated. All solid colors are acceptable in this breed. They stand somewhere between 14 and 15.2hh.

LEFT, ABOVE & OPPOSITE: The Morgan is one of the first horse breeds ever to have been developed in the United States. It is an attractive animal, and often has a long, flowing mane and tail.

PINTO/PAINT HORSE

The Pinto or Paint Horse (from the Spanish *pintado*, meaning "painted"), like many of the old American breeds, is descended from Iberian horses that were brought to the Americas by the conquistadors in the 16th century. They are sometimes referred to as "calico" horses in America.

In England and other Anglophone countries they are referred to as "piebalds" (black-and-white) or "skewbalds" (any other color and white) because their coats, of any solid color, are heavily mottled with white; alternatively they are merely referred to as

colored horses, though in the United States the Pinto is regarded as a separate breed.

The original Spanish horses were allowed to revert to a feral condition and gradually extended into North America, where they roamed the Western deserts. Once domesticated by Native Americans, however, they became greatly revered; in fact, it was believed that the Pinto even possessed magic powers.

Ranchers also adopted these hardy horses, whose stamina and agility made them excellent for work over great distances. Today, they are still used as workhorses but also at rodeos; they are also

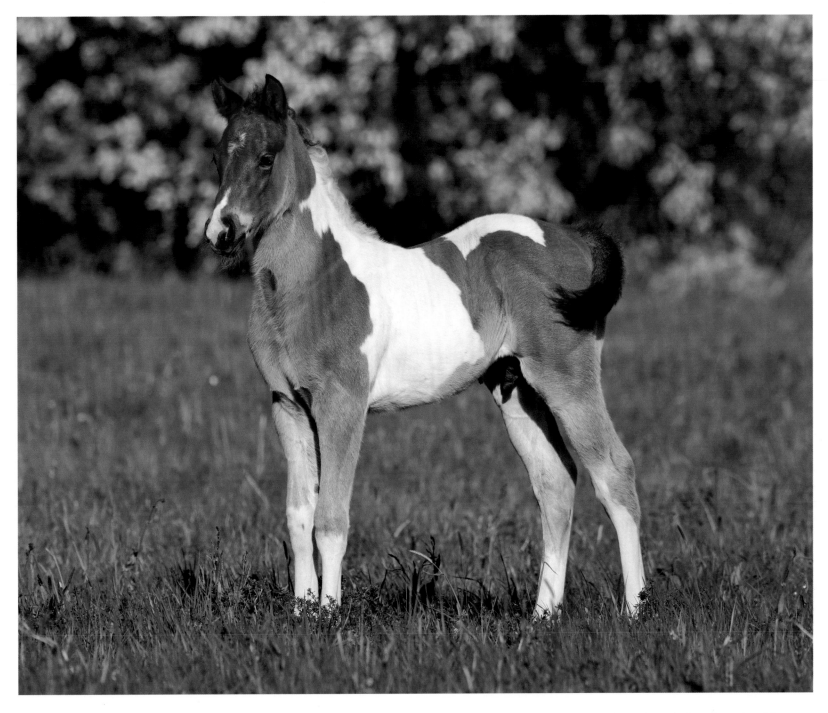

used for trail-riding and showing and as all-round riding horses.

The Pinto has a fine head and graceful, well-defined neck. The ears are alert and of medium length, while the eyes indicate spirit and intelligence. They are usually quite short in the back, with long, strong legs and hard, tough hooves. They are hardy and agile.

The Pinto is well-known for its striking coat, which can be black, chestnut, brown, bay, dun, sorrel, palomino, gray or roan, patched with large areas of white. There are three distinctive types of coat pattern: Tobiano, in which the head is like that of any solid-colored horse, but there are round or oval spots resembling shields running over the neck and chest. One or both flanks may be colored white or a color can predominate, while the tail is often bi-colored; Overo,

which is predominantly dark or white, though the white shouldn't cross the back between withers and tail. The head should be white with scattered irregular markings on the rest of the body. At least one leg should be dark and the tail is usually one color; Tovero is a mixture of the two. Pintos stand between 14.2 and 15.2hh.

THESE PAGES & OVERLEAF: Pintos are useful horses, when it comes to trail-riding and work over great distances, being sure-footed and with plenty of stamina and agility.

PASO FINO

Coming from Puerto Rico, the foundation of the Paso Fino is old Spanish or Iberian stock. It has the same bloodlines, inherited from horses brought to the Americas by the Spanish conquistadors in the 16th century; in terms of character and conformation, however, different environments have caused slight variations in their evolution.

The Paso Fino is a naturally gaited horse, like the Peruvian Paso or Stepping Horse and another lesser-known Colombian breed, and although it is predominantly a working horse, these attributes make it stand out from the crowd. Aficionados claim that because of its natural, even, four-beat gait, that can be performed at varying speeds, it is the smoothest riding horse in the world. The classic *fino* is a collected gait, executed with a rapid footfall that covers little ground.

The *paso corto* is a moderate gait, useful in trail riding, and the *paso largo* is a fast gait in which the horse can reach speeds equivalent to a canter or slow gallop. Not all Paso Finos can perform the classic *fino*, but the majority perform the other gaits with ease.

There are another two variants: the *sobre paso*, a more natural gait in which the horse is allowed a loose rein and is relaxed, and which is used in general riding rather than the show ring; and the *andadura*, which is a fast, pacing gait. This is uncomfortable, however, so it is only performed for short periods. The rest of the time the horse's effortless gait makes riding it extremely comfortable and smooth.

Paso Finos are in great demand for showing and displays. The head is fine, almost Arab-like, with a straight nose and flaring nostrils. It has

longish, well-shaped ears and intelligent eyes. The body is very Spanish, similar to the Andalusian's, with a good sloping shoulder, well-developed neck, and a medium-length back. It has slightly sloping quarters and a low-set tail. The legs are sturdy and strong with large hocks.

The Paso Fino has an excellent temperament and great enthusiasm. Despite its small stature it is very strong; in fact, even the smallest will easily carry a man over hills and rough terrain. It may be any color and stands between 14 and 15hh.

ABOVE, OPPOSITE LEFT & RIGHT: Ancient Iberian bloodlines are still very much in evidence in the Paso Fino.

PONY OF THE AMERICAS

This is a relatively new breed dating from the 1950s and is the result of an accidental cross between a Scottish Shetland Pony and an Appaloosa mare with Arab connections. When the foal, Black Hand I, was born, it was found to be a smaller version of its dam and it was this stallion that became the foundation of America's first pony breed.

The breed has the appearance of a small horse rather than a pony; later on, further refinement was added when Quarter Horse and Arab bloodlines were introduced, producing the showy, high-stepping action so popular in the show ring today.

Similar in stature to British Thoroughbred ponies, the Pony of the Americas is ideal for small children, who find it easy to handle. It is also strong enough to carry a small adult and is used in endurance, trail-riding and showjumping, as well as trotting and pony flat-racing.

The head is very Arab, with a broad forehead, small pricked ears, and a straight or slightly dished nose. The eyes are large and kind. The body is of medium length, with a good sloping shoulder, well-developed quarters, and fine but strong legs. It is strong and hardy, with a calm but willing disposition. It shares similar markings with the Appaloosa, and stands between 11.2 and 14hh.

BELOW & OPPOSITE: Ideally, the Pony of the Americas should display style and substance, beauty and symmetry, being well-balanced and correct in all aspects of its conformation.

QUARTER HORSE

It is no surprise that the Quarter Horse holds pride of place in the hearts of all American horse-lovers, seeing that it was the first breed to become established in the United States.

The Quarter Horse's origins can be traced back 500 years to the time when the Spanish conquistadors brought Iberian and Oriental horses to Florida. English colonists eventually acquired these horses

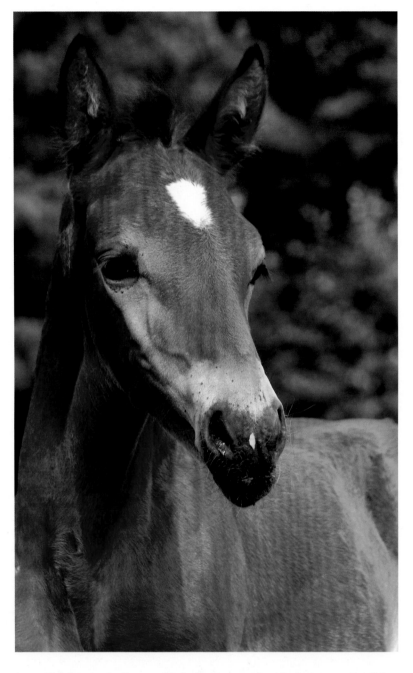

from Chickasaw Indians, which they crossed with their own English horses, mainly Thoroughbreds, then refined them again with more Thoroughbred blood.

Before the days of race tracks, the early colonists used to race their horses down the main street, which was usually about a quarter-of-a-mile long. The name Quarter Horse, therefore, came

LEFT, ABOVE, OPPOSITE: The Quarter Horse comes in two main body types: the stock type and the hunter or racing type. The stock type, although agile, is shorter, more compact, stocky and well-muscled, while the hunter or racing type, bearing more of a resemblance to the Thoroughbred, is somewhat taller and smoother muscled than the stock type.

from the ability of these horses to achieve great speeds over a short distance. The powerful hindquarters of the Quarter Horse gave it great acceleration and even today it is faster than the Thoroughbred over short sprints.

Not only was the Quarter Horse a talented sprinter, it also made a good riding horse, pulled wagons, and was an efficient packhorse. Its most valuable attribute, however, was its natural instinct to round up herds. This undoubtedly had been inherited from its Iberian forebears,

which had nerves of steel and amazing agility. They also had plenty of cow sense, having worked the bullrings of Portugal and Spain for generations. Today, racing predominates, but their use in rodeos, trailing and as all-round family mounts is widespread across the United States, Canada, Australia and even parts of Europe.

Quarter Horses can be quite large animals, due to the influence of the Thoroughbred in their breeding. The head is relatively small and the eyes are bright and set far apart. The neck, hindquarters and back are extremely muscular, which makes the feet appear relatively small.

Quarter Horses are easy to maintain, and are enthusiastic, honest and energetic. Their coats may be of any color, and their height range is between 14.2 and 16hh.

LEFT & BELOW: The Quarter Horse is extremely agile. It is excellent at cutting cattle and are often used in Rodeo events.

STANDARDBRED

The Standardbred is famous for its trotting and pacing abilities and is widely used in harness racing throughout the world. The breed dates back 200 years, when trotting races had become sufficiently popular to warrant a breeding program of their own.

The founding sire of today's Standardbred was Messenger, a gray Thoroughbred, born in 1780 and imported to Philadelphia in 1788. While Messenger was bred for traditional racing at a gallop, his own sire, Mambrino, had been responsible for a long dynasty of famous trotting coachhorses in England.

Messenger worked at stud for about 20 years and became famous for producing strong, talented trotters. Meanwhile, during the mid-1800s in New England, the Morgan breed was being used to produce a line of smaller trotters with a straight up-and-down action. The high-stepping action of the Morgan line was then combined with the long-reaching stride of the Messenger, which increased the performance of the Standardbred no end.

The trot of a Standardbred appears huge in comparison with that of ordinary breeds and is a gait whereby the legs are moved in diagonal pairs. The "pace," however, is peculiar to this breed and is a gait where the horse moves its legs in lateral pairs. While the trot comes naturally to all horses, the pace generally has to be taught, although some Standardbreds seem able to pace from birth. Pacing is quicker than trotting as it allows the stride to be longer and more economical.

The term Standardbred was introduced in 1879 and derives from the time standard that was set to test the ability of harness racers. Originally, the Standardbred horse was required to cover a mile in 2 minutes and 30 seconds. Since this first standard was set, improved breeding has enabled the modern Standardbred to beat this target easily.

The head is in proportion to the horse's body and the eyes are kind, while the ears are indicative of its alertness. The horse is muscular overall, with a well-sprung barrel, sloping shoulder, and a strong back. The legs resemble those of the Thoroughbred, though they are rather more solid, with larger joints; the hooves are large and strong.

The Standardbred has an excellent temperament and is quite a placid horse when away from the race track. When racing, however, it is highly competitive, and displays great stamina and unbounding energy. They come in all solid colors, but mainly bay, black, brown and chestnut. Size ranges from 14.2–17.2hh.

BELOW & OPPOSITE: Standardbreds tend to be more muscled and longer-bodied than Thoroughbreds. They are also more placid, making them more suited to racing, with its attendant strategies and changes of speed.

TENNESSEE WALKING HORSE

The Tennessee (or Plantation) Walking Horse originated in the deep south of the United States and was recognized as the ideal utility breed to carry plantation owners around their large estates. The smooth, gliding gait of the "Walker" (as the breed is also known) provided hours of comfort in the saddle; the movement is performed from the elbow rather than the shoulder, thus transmitting the minimum of movement to the rider. Although still widely ridden for pleasure, the Walker is nowadays extensively bred for the show ring, and it is also used as a general riding and harness horse.

In fact there are two or three characteristic gaits, the flat-footed walk, the running walk, and the canter. The first horse perceived to have this natural talent was foaled in 1837, but it took another 50 years or so to establish the breed as it is today.

The Thoroughbred, Standardbred, American Saddlebred, Narragansett Pacer and Morgan bloodlines all played their part in establishing this distinctive breed, but it was one stallion, born in 1886, that became its foundation stallion. It possessed all the desired qualities, such as the delightful temperament and the characteristic gaits. Most of the offspring inherited their sire's traits and he subsequently enjoyed many successful years at stud. Once a breed association had become established, approximately 300,000 horses were registered.

The Walker has a large head with a straight profile, gentle eyes, and pointed ears. The neck is arched and muscular, with a broad base that enables the head to be carried elegantly high. The breed has plenty of bone, which adds to its sturdiness, and a short-coupled and level topline. The limb joints are well-made, with particularly powerful hocks that allow the hindlegs to step well under the body. The tail, which is usually left long, is often nicked and set artificially high.

Walkers are naturally gentle and calm, but it is their unusual gaits for which they are most famous. Although the gaits are inherited, they need to be developed by further training. The flat walk, running walk and canter are natural to the breed. The running walk has several variations: the rack, the stepping pace, the fox-trot and single-foot.

Tennessee Walking Horses may be any color, but especially black, chestnut, brown, gray, roan or bay. Height is between 15 and 17h.

BELOW & OPPOSITE: The Tennessee Walker is frequently to be seen in programs featuring handicapped riders, and people with back problems often find it a more comfortable horse to ride.

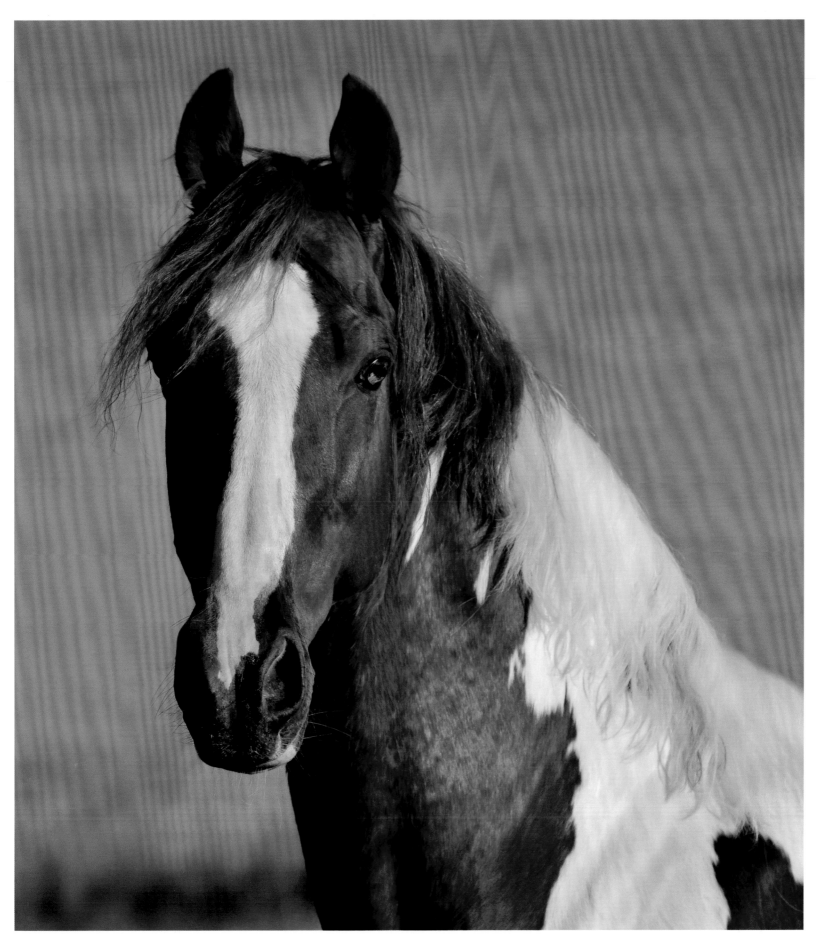

CHAPTER THREE
HORSES OF WESTERN EUROPE

"He's of the colour of the nutmeg. And of the heat of the ginger.... he is pure air and fire; and the dull elements of earth and water never appear in him, but only in patient stillness while his rider mounts him; he is indeed a horse, and all other jades you may call beasts."

—William Shakespeare

ALTÉR REAL

Portugal has two breeds of horses, both of which are used in the bullring and in haute école classical riding: the famous Lusitano (page 144) and the lesser known, but no less noble, Altér Real. The breed had its beginnings in the 18th century, when 300 Andalusian mares, intended for the specific requirements of the Portuguese court in Lisbon, were brought from Jerez in Spain to the royal house of Braganza's stud at Vila de Portel in Portugal. After eight years, the stud moved to Altér do Chão, which gave the horse the first part of its name, the second part meaning royal. For many years the breed

ABOVE, OPPOSITE LEFT & RIGHT: The Altér Real is termed a Baroque horse, being particularly suited to haute école classicism.

excelled not only in classical disciplines but also as a quality carriage horse.

The Altér Real breed came under jeopardy during the Napoleonic invasion of 1809–10, when troops stole the best horses from the stud, drastically reducing their numbers. Then, in 1832, King Miguel abdicated and much of the stud's land became subject to confiscation.

In later years, measures were taken to improve the existing stock by breeding it with Thoroughbreds, Normans and Arabs; this, however, only served to weaken the breed, causing much loss of its original character. In the late 19th century, however, the Spanish Zapata family introduced more Andalusian and Carthusian blood, and this reversed much of the earlier damage.

The breed finally obtained the protection it deserved in the early 20th century, when steps were taken to restore it to its former glory. This was achieved with the help of Dr. Ruy d'Andrade who, with two stallions and a handful of mares, founded a top-quality Altér Real stud. He eventually handed the stud over to the Portuguese Ministry of Agriculture, which administers the breeding program today. The Altér Real is still used in haute école and general riding.

The head has all the distinctive Iberian qualities of the Lusitano and Andalusian, having a fine head with a slightly dished nose, medium-length shapely ears, and a lively, intelligent eye. The neck is

short but well-positioned, with a pronounced, arched crest. The shoulders are sloping and the chest is well-developed. The back is short and strong with ample quarters. The legs are hard and very tough, the upper parts being well-muscled with large joints ending in small but well-shaped hooves.

The Altér Real has a high-stepping action which is most attractive: this, coupled with its strength and power, makes it appear much larger than it actually is. Unlike its Iberian brothers, the Altér Real is not suitable for beginners in that it has inherited a fiery and lively temperament from non-Iberian blood added in the early 19th century. It is responsive and learns quickly but needs a competent and experienced rider in order to excel. Coat color is usually bay and height is between 15 and 16hh.

ANDALUSIAN

This celebrated Spanish breed is one of the oldest to have been handled and ridden by man: there is further evidence of this fact in cave paintings, which confirm that horses of this kind were present in the Iberian Peninsula in around 5000 BC.

The Andalusian's lineage stems from the Sorraia Pony, which still exists in Iberia, and the North African Barb, with additional Arab and Oriental strains. It evolved in Iberia, most of which was then known as Andalusia, at the time of the Moorish occupation of 711. The result was a horse with a head-carriage that was high and proud, and paces that were extravagant and highly placed.

THESE PAGES & OVERLEAF: The Andalusian is one of the purest breeds of horses present in the world today. It shares similarities with the closely related Lusitano breed.

The Andalusian was particularly valued as a warhorse, having all the qualities that enabled it to perform well in battle. (It is interesting to note that El Cid's mount, Babieca, was an Andalusian.) Later, in the 16th century, the conquistadors brought the horse with them to the Americas, where it became the basis of all American breeds, which also share lineage with the Lusitano, Carthusian and Altér Real.

OPPOSITE & BELOW: Andalusians are proud horses that are full of courage.

The Andalusian bloodline is evident in around 80 percent of modern breeds and has had a particular influence on the Connemara, native to Ireland, the Lipizzaner of the Balkans, and the Cleveland Bay and Welsh Cob of the British Isles. However, its popularity was not to last, and in around 1700 the Andalusian's heavy, robust conformation fell from favor, when lighter, sleeker animals, used for hunting and racing, became more fashionable. Andalusians suffered even more when a plague and famine almost wiped them out; a few survived in the Carthusian monasteries of

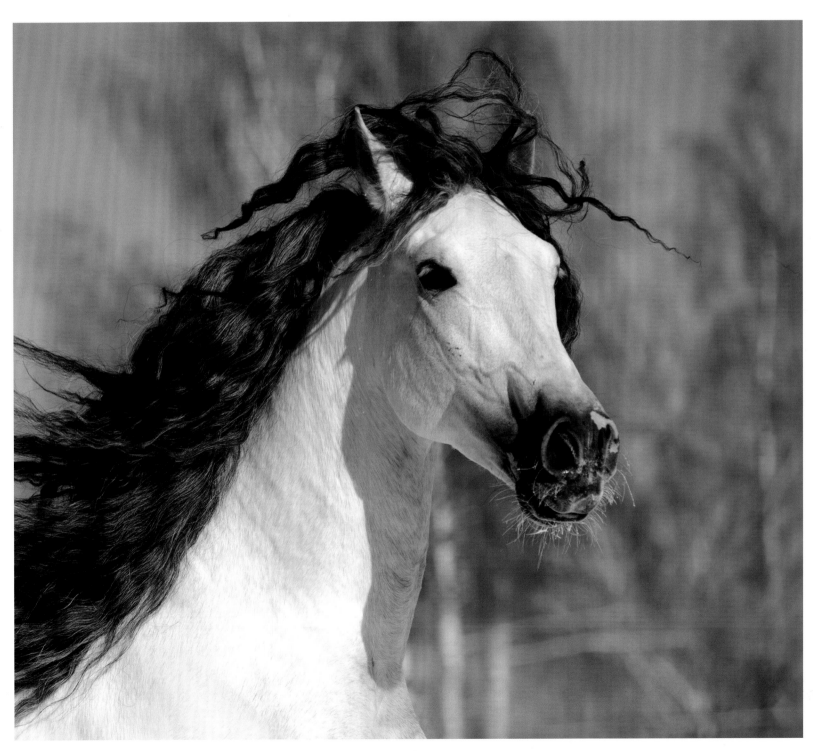

Castello, Jerez and Seville, where breeding from the best of the animals continued.

Today, the Andalusian can still be traced back to these lines, the purest and most beautiful of which are still referred to as *caballos Cartujanos*. Their extreme rarity forced the Spanish government to ban their export for over 100 years, but the embargo was lifted in the 1960s, and they now enjoy popularity around the world.

Today, the Andalusian is used for bullfighting and display riding, where its power and agility allow it to execute the intricate movements with ease. They excel at advanced classical dressage and at showjumping and are also useful for general riding and driving. They are often to be seen in hand in the show ring.

These muscular horses have great presence and beauty. The neck is heavy, with a well-developed crest. The mane is abundant and should be kept long. The head-carriage is noble and high, the forehead wide with expressive, medium-length ears. The eyes are dark-brown and gentle, the nostrils are flared, and the jaw is large and well-muscled. The withers are well-rounded and the shoulder is long and sloping. The chest is broad, the croup rounded, and the low-set tail is thick and long. The body is rounded and short-coupled, adding to the overall strength. The legs are strong with large joints and the hooves are rounded and compact.

The Andalusian is famous for its extravagant paces. Movement is elevated and extended, making the horse look as if it were floating on air. All paces are smooth, showy and spectacular.

Andalusians are proud and courageous, and although spirited to ride, they have amiable temperaments. They have soft mouths, making them extremely obedient when ridden correctly.

Gray and bay coats are most in evidence, but others are accepted by the Andalusian Horse Association. In Spain, according to the studbook, only gray, bay and black are acceptable. Height is between 15 and 16.2hh.

OPPOSITE & ABOVE: The Andalusian was originally a prized warhorse, said to have been used by El Cid as well as Napoleon's armies.

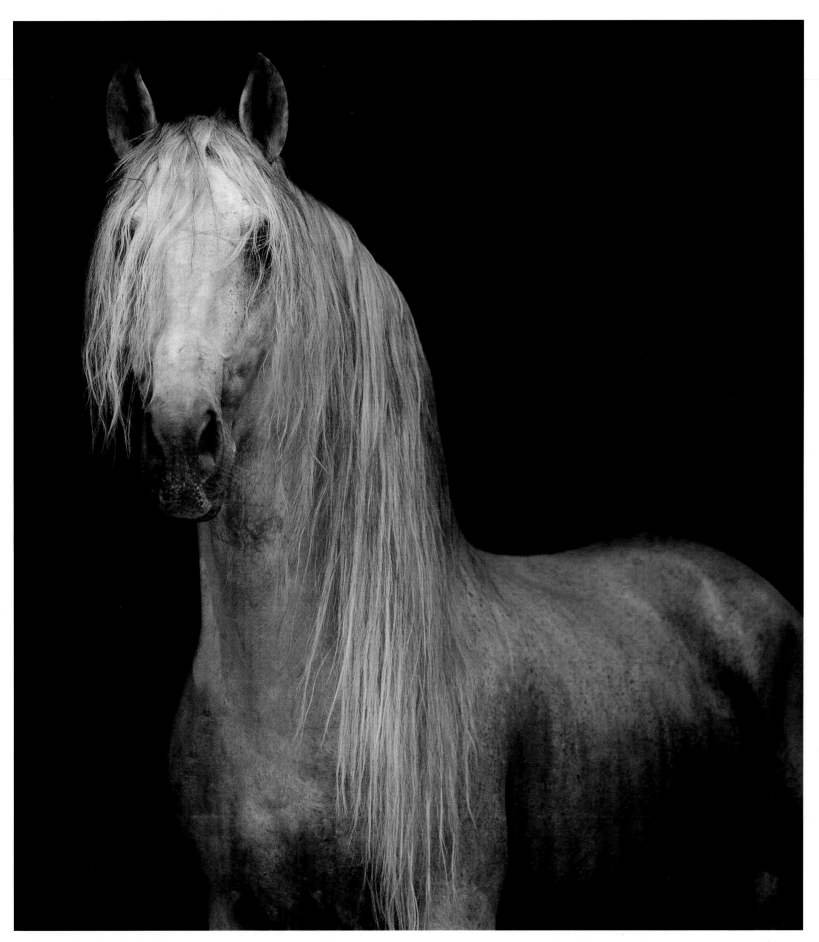

ANGLO-ARAB

The Anglo-Arab derives its name from two of the world's greatest breeds, the Thoroughbred, which is of English (Anglo) origin, and the Arab. The rules of Anglo-Arab breeding in the United Kingdom are very strict, and only these two bloodlines can be present. Other countries have their own rules, with some adding elements of their own native breeds, the French Anglo-Arab being such a one. There are other stipulations, however, and at least 25 percent Arab content is the norm.

Because the Anglo-Arab is a mixture of two breeds it is not actually recognized as such, with one exception: the fore-mentioned

LEFT, ABOVE & OPPOSITE: The exciting blend of Thoroughbred and Arab combines the superior speed of the Thoroughbred with the better temperament of the Arabian.

French Anglo-Arab. There are other variations which appear all over Europe, the Gidrán or Hungarian Anglo-Arab, the Shagya Arab, also from Hungary, the Russian Strelets-Arab, and Spain's Hispano-Arab.

Anglo-Arabs make superb riding horses and excel in most disciplines, including showjumping, eventing and dressage. They also do well in riding-horse showing classes, where, unlike the pure Arab, which must be left as it is, their manes and tails can be plaited. The combination of the Thoroughbred's complaisant nature and the strength, stamina and intelligence of the Arab make an ideal combination.

The interesting thing about breeding Anglo-Arabs is that one never know how they are going to turn out: they can be either predominantly Arab or Thoroughbred, or a combination of both; either way they are ideal all-rounders and extremely rewarding to ride.

The Anglo-Arab should have the skeletal structure and conformation of the Thoroughbred and the tail and head-carriage of the Arab, though this can occasionally vary, with some having lighter bones than others. The head should have unmistakable Arab features, with a dished or straight profile that is not quite as extreme as the

Arab's. The eyes should indicate that the horse can be spirited on occasions, while the nostrils are large and flared. The ears are medium-sized, fine, pointed and expressive. The head-carriage is fairly high, with a well-developed crest. The Anglo-Arab should have the good sloping shoulders, deep chest and powerful hindquarters of the Thoroughbred. The tail-carriage can be either high like the Arab's or lower as in the Thoroughbred.

Anglo-Arabs are usually affectionate and intelligent. They are also brave and spirited and will always give of their very best. The most usual colors are brown, bay, chestnut and gray, while black is rather more rare. There is often white on the face and legs, but never on the rest of the body. Anglo-Arabs stand somewhere between 14.2 and 16.1hh.

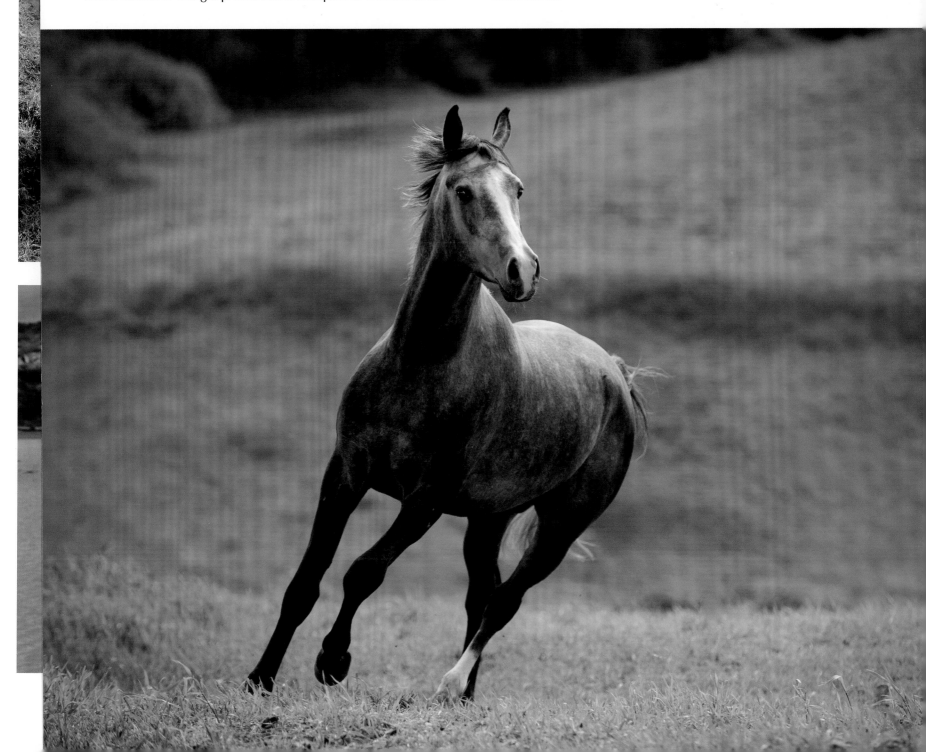

DARTMOOR

There is evidence to suggest that ponies inhabited Dartmoor as early as 2000 BC, a fact confirmed by remains excavated on Shaugh Moor. The earliest written reference to the Dartmoor is in the will of Awifold of Credition, who died in 1012. The breed stems from the Celtic Pony which went on to breed with other British natives; later, there were additions of Roadster, Welsh Pony, Cob, Arab, and in recent times, Thoroughbred.

The Dartmoor pony comes from the county of Devon in the south-west of England and gets its name from the area of wild moorland which it still roams. Standing over 1,000ft (305m) above sea level, with wind and rain driving off the sea, it is at times an inhospitable place, with rocky outcrops and sparse vegetation. Consequently, the pony is extremely hardy and sure-footed and has plenty of stamina.

Dartmoors fail to thrive if left solely to their own devices, however, and require extra hay in winter, which farmers put out for

THESE PAGES & OVERLEAF: In medieval times, Dartmoor Ponies were used to carry heavy loads of tin across the moor; but when the mines were closed, they were allowed to roam free.

them. This was confirmed during the Second World War when Dartmoor was completely out of bounds. As a result, the population dwindled to only two stallions and 12 mares because of the lack of supplementary feeding. Nowadays the breed has been greatly improved and with careful monitoring is now flourishing. Children like to ride Dartmoors and they are also used for showing and driving.

The Dartmoor has a small, nicely-set neat head, with small, alert ears and an intelligent and kindly eye. The neck is of medium length and fairly well-developed, as are the back, loins and quarters.

The tail is high-set, the legs are shapely but sturdy, and the hooves are well-formed and hard.

Dartmoors make excellent children's ponies, and their small size makes them easily manageable. They also have kind and docile natures.

The Dartmoor's most striking feature is that it moves with almost no knee flexion: this produces a long, free-flowing stride similar to that of a horse and is very comfortable for the rider. Dartmoors are mainly bay and brown with only a little white on the legs and face. Height is up to 12.2hh.

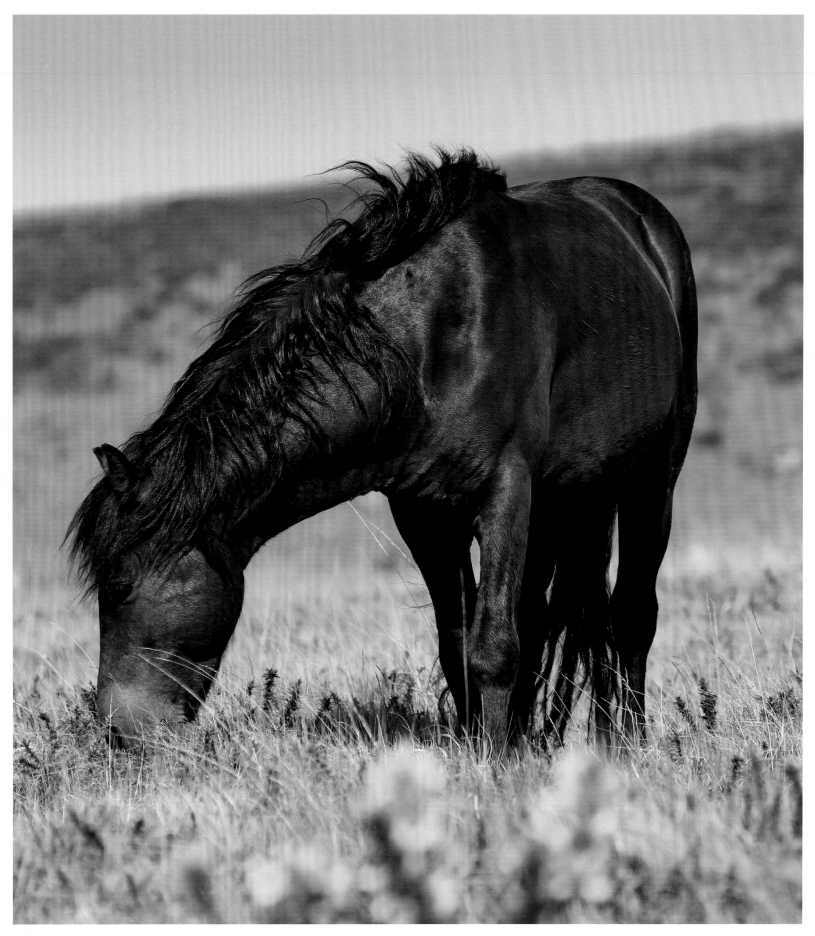

EXMOOR

The Exmoor is truly ancient, said to have existed before the last Ice Age when similar ponies migrated south from Alaska, and where bones matching those of the modern pony have been found. Exmoor's isolated position, covering remote areas of the counties of Devon and Somerset in England, has ensured that very little cross-breeding has occurred, which has maintained the purity of the breed; indeed, the Exmoor pony is one of the purest breeds in the world, unlike its near cousin, the Dartmoor, which, having been more accessible to other

BELOW & RIGHT: The Exmoor is a rare and unique survivor. Attempts to breed it outside of its natural state have met with little success, causing breeders constantly to return to the wild herds for feral blood.

influences, has been subjected to more evolutions. Exmoors are truly wild ponies and they still live up on the moors. Being regarded as a rare breed, with only 1,000 ponies worldwide, they are now closely monitored. There are aproximately 300 breeding mares in the U.K., producing around 130 foals a year. Half of these mares still live on Exmoor and to protect the purity of the breed each foal is inspected, numbered and branded with the society's mark on the flank and the herd number on the shoulder.

Various farms in the area are involved in the breeding of the Exmoor ponies, with the result that their future is now much brighter. Nowadays, Exmoors are also being bred in other parts of Britain, but the moors ponies are still used as foundation stock to ensure the purity of the breed.

The Exmoor's head is large, with a broad forehead and hooded eyes (known as "toad-eyes") to protect them from the elements. The ears are thick and short and the nose is straight. The neck is also thick and well-developed, with a deep chest; the short, fine legs are

nevertheless muscular, with a little feathering around the fetlocks. The hooves are small and hard. The coat is dense with a thick, wiry mane and tail.

Exmoors are extremely tough and can live out all-year-round. If they are to be domesticated, they must be caught and broken in while young. They are good-natured, willing and obedient and make good children's ponies.

Exmoors can be bay, brown or dun with black points. There should be no white, but the distinctive mealy markings should be present around the eyes, muzzle and flanks. Mares should not exceed 12.2hh or stallions 12.3hh.

BELOW & OPPOSITE: The ancient Exmoor breed is now rare, with around 1,000 ponies existing worldwide. There are still herds living up on the wild stretches of Exmoor National Park.

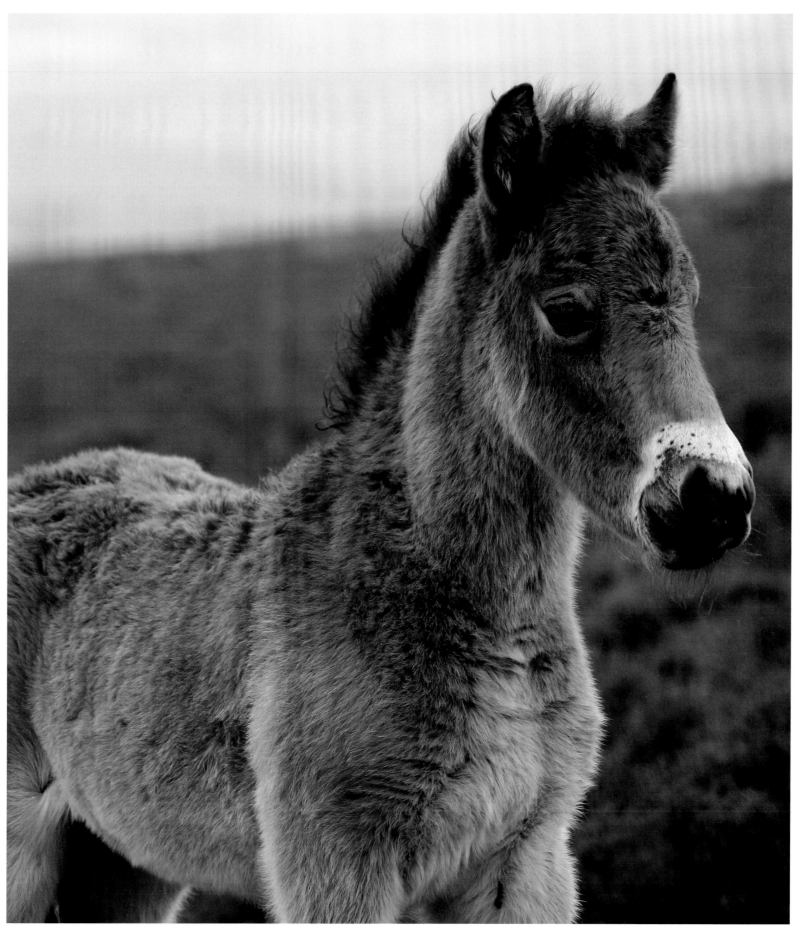

FELL

The Fell is closely related to the Dales Pony, though it originated on the western side of the Pennines, inhabiting the hills and mountains of Cumbria in north-eastern England. It is a descendant of the Celtic Pony, that once roamed much of northern Europe, and which the Romans used as draft animals and in raids against the Picts. They were later used by reivers – the cattle-raiders of the Scottish Border country – because they were known to be sure-footed and with plenty of stamina.

The Fell's checkered history became more eventful when they were used by smugglers around Britain's northern coast. They were also bred by Cistercian monks, who introduced gray ponies to signify that they belonged to the monastery.

Over the years, and like the Dales, the breed was improved by mating with other stock, such as the Friesian, to which the Fell bears a resemblance. It remains much purer then the Dales, however, which has been subjected to rather more added bloodstock.

Like many native breeds, numbers declined during and after the two world wars, when farms switched to machinery and motorized

BELOW & OPPOSITE: Because the Fell Pony runs very true to type, it is that much easier to find matched pairs for driving.

OPPOSITE & ABOVE: Vikings used the ponies for plowing and sled-pulling, the Normans for shepherding, and by the 13th century, Fells were hauling goods in Belgium's thriving wool industry.

transport as they became more readily available. The Fell, however, remained popular as a riding and driving pony and its fortunes have been happily reversed. Today, the Fell is an all-round family pony, strong enough to carry an adult and docile enough for children to ride. They make excellent trekking ponies, making them popular with the tourist industry. They are also used in harness and are still occasionally used to herd sheep.

The Fell bears a strong resemblance to the Friesian. The head is noble, with a broad forehead and a straight or slightly dished, tapering nose, with large flaring nostrils. The eyes are proud and intelligent and the ears small and neat. The head sits well on the neck, which is of medium length, strong but not overdeveloped. The shoulders are well-muscled and sloping, ensuring a good smooth action. The body is sturdy with a strong back and deep chest. The legs are strong and muscular, with fine feathering present on the backs of the legs; the hooves are well-shaped and are the characteristic blue color. Mane and tail should not be trimmed but left to grow naturally.

The Fell Pony has an excellent constitution and like most mountain and moorland ponies it is hardy and able to live out all-year-round. It is easy-going and enjoys the company of humans beings; it is a free spirit, however, and can be willful on occasions. Fell Ponies are famous for their excellent paces, which make them comfortable to ride. They excel at endurance events and are fast into the bargain, which is an asset in harness.

Fells are usually pure black with no white markings, but bay, gray and brown are also possible. A small amount of white is permissable around the fetlocks or in the form of a small star on the forehead. They stand around 14hh.

FJORD

The Norwegian Fjord is most likely descended from the Przewalski or Asiatic Wild Horse, which in turn was descended from Ice Age horses. It seems to have retained many of its ancestors' characteristics, including the pale coat, the dorsal stripe down the back, and the occasional zebra stripes on the legs, which were typical of the ancient breed.

The primitive breed was improved over many hundreds of years by breeding with the Celtic Pony and Tarpan. The result has been utilized for thousands of years, and there is evidence of its use in raids and battles from Viking artifacts. The Vikings had a particularly bloodthirsty approach to selection: they allowed stallions to fight to the death, ensuring that the stronger specimens continued the breed.

Fjords still have their manes clipped in the manner seen on Viking rune stones; the mane is unusual in that the hair is cream on the outer edges and black in the center, being a part of the

THESE PAGES & OVERLEAF: All breeding in Norway is now under government control, and only champion stock can be exported. Fjords now have registries in the U.S., Canada and elsewhere. Twenty-two Fjords have been imported to the U.S., most of them in the 1950s.

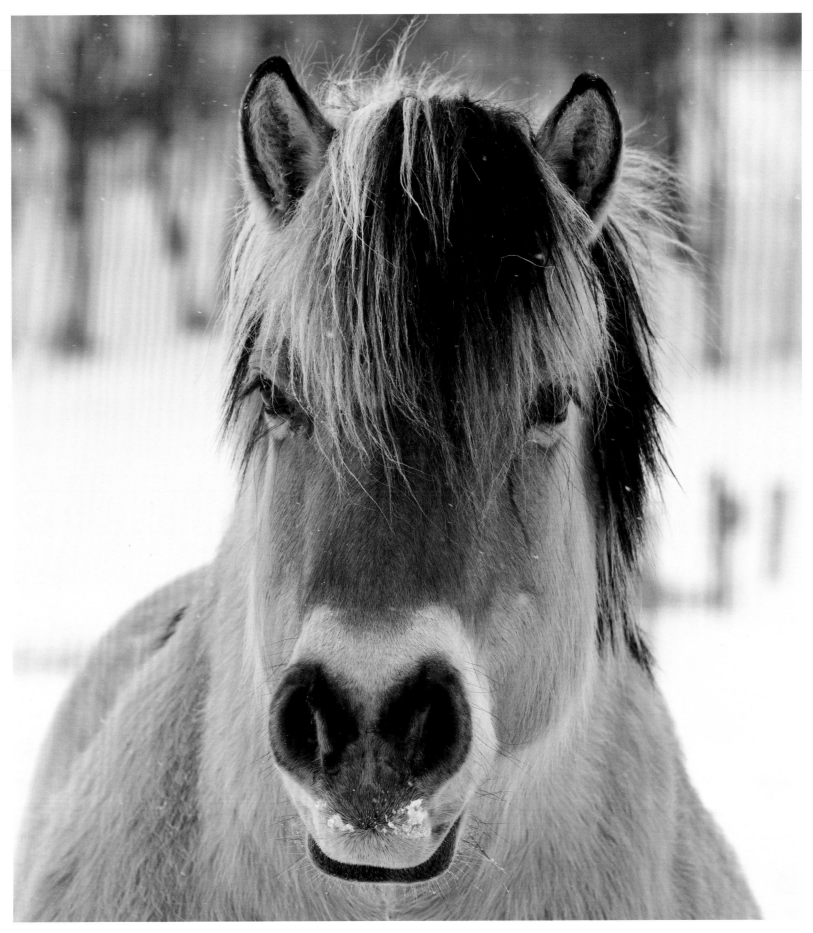

dorsal stripe. The mane is therefore clipped so that the black part remains prominent.

The Fjord has been used to improve many other Northern European breeds, including the Icelandic and Highland. Today they can be seen over most of Scandinavia, mainly as children's riding ponies. The Fjord is sure-footed and excellent at trekking and long-distance endurance events. It is also popular in harness, where it has been successful in competition. Some are still used around the farm for light plowing and as packhorses.

The Fjord has an attractive head: it is short and wide with short, neat ears, a slightly dished face and large nostrils. The eyes are large and kind, and the neck is short and thick, accentuated by the traditionally clipped mane. The body is sturdy, with sloping quarters and a low-set tail. The legs are strong with plenty of bone and the feet are tough and hard.

All Fjords are dun-colored, which is a body color that is a tan, gold or a related shade with darker (usually black or dark brown) points and primitive markings. White markings are discouraged, though a small star is acceptable. Some also have zebra stripes on the legs. The hooves are most often dark, but can be a lighter brown color on lighter-colored horses. Fjords stand between 13.2 and 14.2hh.

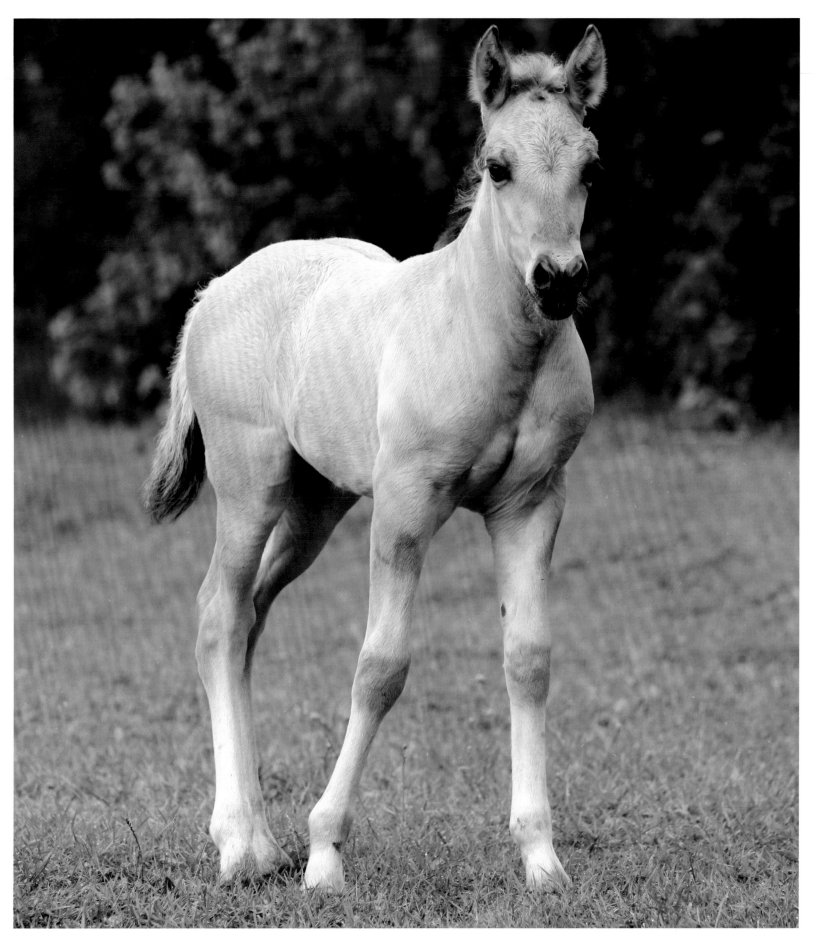

FRENCH TROTTER

The first race track used for trotting in France opened in Cherbourg in 1839, and the sport has never looked back since then. The first races were a means of selecting suitable stallions and became quite an event. The most popular trotters at that time were Norman and Anglo-Norman breeds; later, these were crossed with Norfolk Roadsters from Britain, and by the end of the 19th century the breed had been further enhanced by infusions of British Hackney, Orlov Trotter from Russia, and Thoroughbred. These breeds did much to create a popular and much respected trotter, and a later addition of American Standardbred seems to have completed the breed.

In 1906 a stud book was created for French Trotters, though the breed itself wasn't recognized as such until 1922. To be acceptable for registration it was necessary that the horse be able to trot .62 mile (1km) in I minute 42 seconds. This was later extended to include only horses whose parents had both been registered, thus ensuring the purity of the breed. Recently, however, even more infusions of Standardbred have been made to improve the breed and its paces; the result is a world-class trotting horse, said to be able to surpass the Standardbred itself. Although there have been infusions of American Standardbred blood, the French Trotter has retained its unusual habit of trotting on the diagonal rather than adopting the lateral pacing of the Standardbred.

Today French Trotters are predominantly used in the sport for which they were bred, both under saddle and in harness; but they also make good riding horses and even jumpers. The horses that have been bred for riding have also been used to sire competition horses – the Selle Français in particular.

In appearance, the French Trotter's Thoroughbred ancestry is much in evidence in the noble head, broad forehead, medium-sized far-apart ears, and kind, intelligent eyes. The nostrils are large and flaring. The neck is long and well-developed, with a straight shoulder, deep chest, and well-formed, powerful quarters. The legs are muscular with plenty of bone and well-shaped hooves.

The French Trotter has all the fine characteristics of the Thoroughbred. It has a good turn of speed, plenty of stamina, and a kind and even temperament, though it is not without spirit. The harness horses are usually a little smaller and lighter than the ridden types. Like the Thoroughbred, all solid colors can be seen, with the occasional roan. Grays are quite rare. Trotters stand at around 16.2hh.

BELOW & OPPOSITE: Bred mainly in Normandy, most French breeders have no more than two or three mares and they often breed, school, train and race their horses themselves.

FRIESIAN

The Friesian is the Netherlands' only surviving indigenous breed. It is descended from a native breed that once roamed Friesland – the western part of the ancient region of Frisia – 3,000 years ago, and where the remains of a similar coldblooded horse have been found. As riding horses, the Friesian's history is an ancient one, with evidence that it was used by Roman soldiers when they were building Hadrian's Wall in around AD 150; this is supported by the fact that Fell and Dales breeds, native to the English Pennines, are also descended from Friesian stock. Friesian bloodlines are also present in the Orlov Trotter and in most American trotters.

Over the years, the original, rather heavy and plain breed was infused with Oriental and Andalusian blood; this improved the breed to such an extent that during the 17th century, Friesians could be seen performing haute école alongside Spanish horses, and Friesians were in demand as elegant carriage horses. During the 19th century, however, the Friesian became something of a rarity, being almost exclusively restricted to Friesland, where it was used as a general riding horse and trotter. By the end of the First World War, the

OPPOSITE & ABOVE: A feature of the Friesian horse is its long mane and tail. When showing, these are not cut and the tail often brushes the ground.

Friesian was in dire peril of extinction, with only three stallions and a few mares still in existence. Fortunately, with careful breeding and an infusion of Oldenburg blood, the Friesian is once again flourishing; today, it is in evidence all over the world – admired for its noble presence and expressive trot, which is particularly striking in harness. It is still used in haute école disciplines.

From the latter part of the 20th century until the present, demand for purebred Friesians, particularly the "modern," finer-boned, taller, more agile version of the breed, increased, so breeders have produced both purebreds and a lighter-weight crossbred horse with valued characteristics, resulting in the Friesian cross and the Friesian Sporthorse.

The head is proud and of medium size, with small, alert ears pointing slightly inward. The eyes are kindly and expressive, the head-carriage is high and elegant, and the neck is of medium length with a high crest. The withers are well-developed, tapering into the back muscles, and the shoulders sloping. The back is of medium length, strong and straight, leading to well-developed loins and quarters. The legs are clean and strong with slight feathering, and the mane and tail are long and luxuriant; when showing, mane and tail should be left untrimmed. The Friesian has a proud bearing and is gentle and amenable if rather energetic. It is always black, and only the smallest of stars is permitted on the forehead. Usually Friesians stand around 15–15.2hh, but some Friesians have been bred larger, reaching more than 16hh.

ABOVE & RIGHT: The Friesian is an ancient breed, dating back 3,000 years, which has been gradually improved to produce a striking animal capable of performing classical dressage.

FURIOSO

As a breed, the Hungarian Furioso has existed for only about 150 years. It was developed by Hungary's famous Mezöhegyes Stud, which was founded by the Habsburg Emperor Joseph II in 1785; it is also where the Nonius was bred.

In 1840 the stud imported an English Thoroughbred called Furioso, and in 1843 another, North Star, which was a Norfolk Roadster. They mated these two with Nonius and Arab mares, the result being two very distinctive breeds, the Furioso and the North Star. By 1885, however, the two breeds had merged to such an extent that only one breed remained, with Furioso traits predominating.

Historically, the Hungarian Csikos herdsmen trained their horses to do many things to help them to survive in their day-to-day working lives, such as training their horses to lie down to protect themselves from the elements and enemies as well as allowing the herdsmen to stand in the saddle in order to keep track of their herds.

Today the Furioso is used as an all-round riding horse and excellent jumper, and its remarkable stamina makes it a highly competent steeplechaser.

The Furioso is a quality horse and possesses all the attributes of its Thoroughbred forebears. The head is fine, with a straight nose leading to a squarish muzzle. The ears are medium-length and shapely, and the eyes are inquisitive and bold. The neck is long and elegant, with fine sloping shoulders; the girth is deep and the legs are long and strong. The quarters are well-developed with a high tail-carriage. Most noticeable is the action of the high-stepping knee, which is inherited from the Nonius. The Furioso makes an elegant carriage horse as well as a riding horse; it has the amenability of the Thoroughbred, together with its spirit and courage.

Furiosos are usually brown, black or bay, with only the minimum of white markings. They stand at around 16.1hh.

LEFT: During the Second World War, the Mezöhegyes-bred Furiosos were thought to have been destroyed, but were renewed from stock discovered in the Hungarian countryside. Besides Hungary and Romania, Furiosos are also bred in Bulgaria and the former Yugoslavia.

GYPSY VANNER

The origins of the Gypsy Vanner or Cob or Drummer Horse, lie with the Irish Travelers, or Gypsies, of the British Isles. The relationship between Gypsies and horses goes back hundreds of years, but it was only some 50 years ago that the horse came to be regarded as a special breed. Until recently, the Irish Cob or traditional colored cob was considered to be more of a type than a breed, until finally, in 1996, it was recognized and registered as such.

Crossed with Friesian, Shire, Dales Pony and Clydesdale, it is now a heavy horse, variable in size and appearance.

The Gypsy Vanner's build is powerful and compact. It should have a "sweet head," meaning that the head is in proportion with the

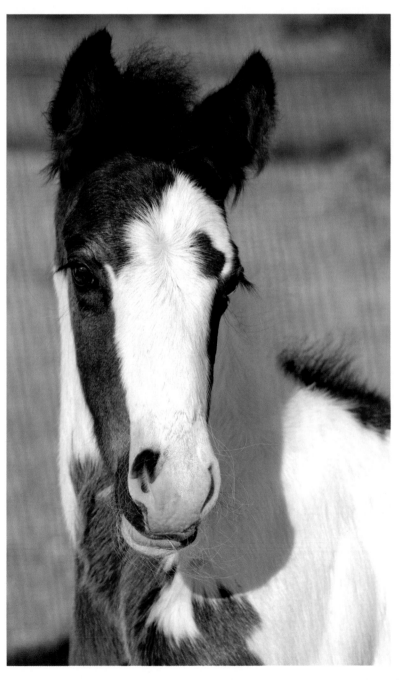

rest of the body. It has an abundant mane and plenty of feathering. The chest should be broad and the withers rounded; the knees should be large and flat and the hooves substantial.

Although known for its extreme docility, the horse is also intelligent and athletic; it must be sound enough, both mentally and physically, to endure a lifetime on the road. It comes in all colors, including piebald and skewbald, and stands between 14 and 15.2hh.

THESE PAGES & OVERLEAF: Gypsy Vanner is the American term for the Irish Cob or piebald horse, also known in parts of Europe as the Irish Tinker Horse, although "tinker" is regarded as a derogatory word and is no longer used. The larger type, that can reach 16hh, is also known as the Drummer Horse, though its connections with the cavalry are tenuous to say the least.

HAFLINGER

The history of the Haflinger is obscure and there are various opinions as to its true origins. It is thought to have come from the South Tyrol in Austria, close to its border with Italy; borders have changed many times throughout history, however, making the exact location impossible to pinpoint. The Haflinger is not unlike the slightly larger Italian Avelignese, and the two probably had common ancestors.

The Haflinger may have been the result of native stock breeding with Oriental horses, which were left behind when the Ostrogoths were driven north by the Byzantine forces in the 6th century AD.

Another story is that King Louis IV of Germany gave a Burgundian stallion to his son as a wedding gift, which was mated with local mares of Oriental origin to produce the Haflinger breed; either way it would seem that Oriental bloodlines are present.

What is known for sure, however, is that the modern Haflinger breed was improved in 1868 when the Arab stallion, El-Bedavi XXII,

THESE PAGES and OVERLEAF: The attractive, versatile Haflinger is fast becoming popular in North America. The primary objective of the American Haflinger Registry is to keep the breed pure.

was imported to the region and bred with Haflinger mares; today, all Haflingers are related to this one stallion.

Today the Haflinger is still to be found in Austria, where it is closely monitored, not only in government-organized breeding programs but also by private individuals. The breed is popular the world over, particularly in Europe, where it is used in the forests and farms of the Tyrol. It is also useful in harness, and as a children's riding pony and family pet.

The Arab influence can be clearly seen in the Haflinger's fine head, which presents a sharp contrast to the stocky body. The nose is slightly dished and the eyes are large and attentive. The ears are small and alert and the nostrils and muzzle neat. The neck is well-proportioned, with fine sloping shoulders, good withers, and a deep girth. The body is broad and strong, with muscular quarters and a high-set tail. Legs are of medium length with tough hooves.

The Haflinger has rhythmic, ground-covering gaits. The walk is relaxed but energetic, and the trot and canter are elastic, energetic, and athletic with a natural tendency to be light on the forehand and balanced. There is some knee action, and the canter has a very distinct motion forward and upward.

The Haflinger is a sociable animal and enjoys the company of people. It is intelligent, trustworthy and docile, making it an excellent work pony and safe with children. Haflingers are hardy and require only moderate feeding; but they do require shelter from cold winds and wet weather. Their most striking feature is their flaxen mane and tail that are usually left long.

Various shades of chestnut, liver or red are permitted, sometimes with a little dappling over paler areas. Height is around 14hh.

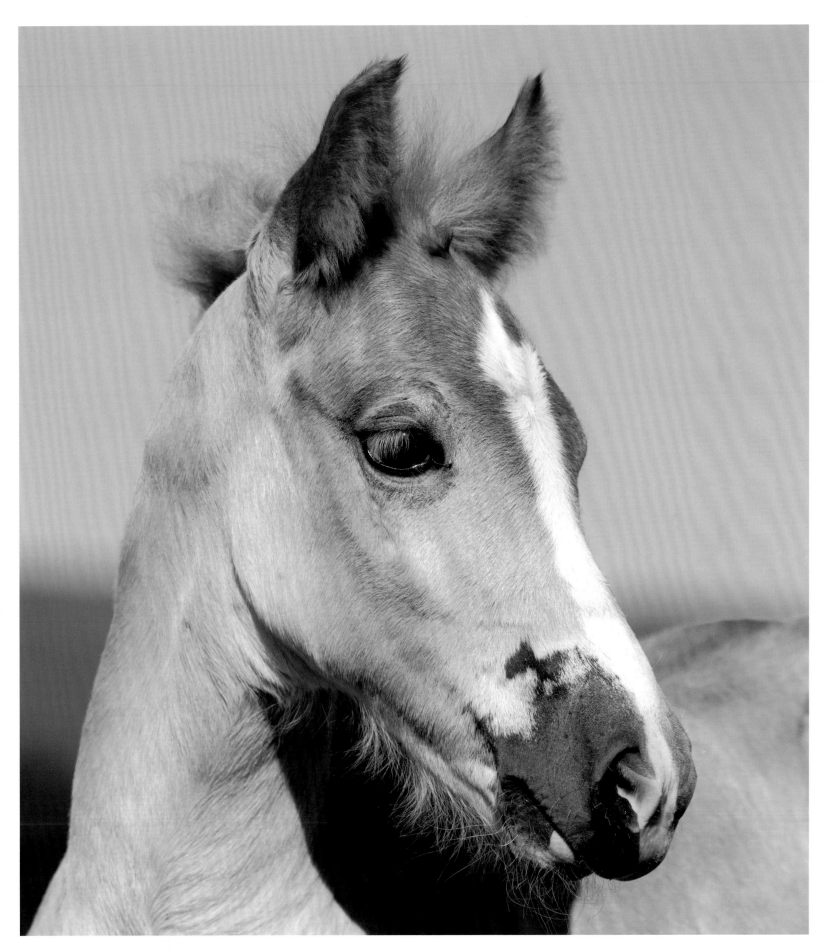

HANOVERIAN

The German Hanoverian horse has a long history. The earliest reference to it as a warhorse was in the 8th century, when Charles Martel frustrated the advances of the Saracens at the Battle of Poitiers. These heavy warhorses were probably a mixture of native, Spanish and Oriental influences.

Hanoverians owe their evolution to warfare, and by the Middle Ages had developed into large, cobby horses, capable of carrying a knight clad in full armor. The type was favored for many centuries until changes in warfare techniques meant that a lighter horse was eventually required. At this time, the Hanoverian was still a heavy breed, even though it was somewhat taller and more agile than a cob; by the 17th century, three distinctive types were being bred for military purposes: Hanoverian, Mecklenburg and Danish horses.

But it was in the 18th century that the Hanoverian truly came into its own, when a member of the House of Hanover, in the person of George I, ascended the British throne in 1714. He spent much of

ABOVE & RIGHT: There are few breeds whose ancestry has been so well-recorded. This has allowed breeders to trace bloodlines over many generations, improving the chances of finding the most promising breeding pairs.

his reign in Hanover, however, and for the next 100 years or so the Hanoverian was nurtured and improved. English Thoroughbred stallions were bred with Hanoverian mares, and Cleveland Bay bloodlines were also added to produce a horse that was still relatively heavy but also suitable for farm use and coachwork.

It was George II who established the state stud at Celle in 1735, where horses for agriculture, riding and driving were bred. Here the Hanoverian breed was improved still further, with additions of Trakehner and Thoroughbred blood; the Hanoverian breed registry was founded in 1888. This horse was very similar to today's famous competition horse.

Probably the best known of all the warmbloods, the modern Hanoverian excels in top dressage and showjumping the world over. Nowadays, the Society of Breeders of the Hanoverian Warmblood Horse is responsible for the purity of the breed. Approximately 160 Hanoverians, mostly stallions, are kept by the state and based at Celle, where they are subjected to tests that assess soundness, conformation

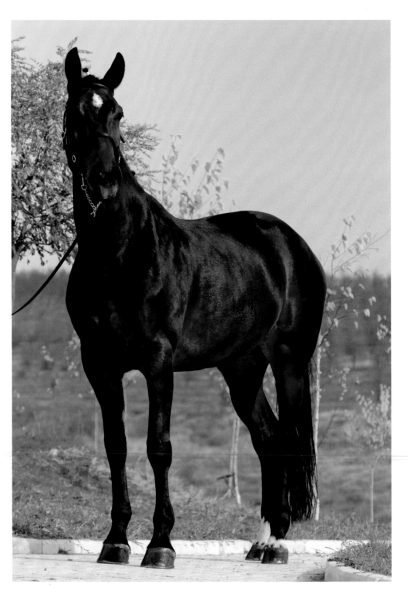

and character for several months before they are allowed to mate.

The Hanoverian has played a large part in the improvement and formation of other warmblood breeds, such as Westphalian, Mecklenburg and Brandenburg horses. Hanoverians now come in two types: the heavier horses are used for showjumping, while the lighter ones, which have more of the Thoroughbred in their make-up, are used for dressage.

The Hanoverian is near-perfect in conformation and its Thoroughbred characteristics are immediately discernible. The head is of medium size, with a straight nose and keen, alert eyes and pricked ears. The neck has a graceful arch and is long and muscular, while the chest is well-developed with a deep girth and sloping shoulder. The back is of medium length, with muscular loins and powerful quarters. The legs are strong with large joints, ending in well-shaped hooves.

The most important feature of the Hanoverian, and one of the crucial tests that stallions have to undergo at Celle, is one of character: only horses with an even temperament and a willing disposition are allowed to breed. Hanoverians are noble and proud, with an excellent free-flowing action which allows them to excel at advanced dressage. They come in all solid colors, often with white on the face and legs. They range in height from 15.2–17hh.

LEFT, ABOVE & OPPOSITE: The Hanoverian, when it was substantially heavier, was a highly-revered warhorse.

HIGHLAND

Like all Scottish native breeds, the Highland has a very ancient lineage, as indicated by its distinctive dorsal stripe. The foundation breed is Celtic Pony, mixed over the centuries with Galloway – now sadly extinct – plus various European breeds, such as Percheron, Spanish, Barb and Clydesdale. In the 19th century Arab was also added to bring the pony up to today's exacting standards.

The pony is not only native to the Highlands, there is also a smaller variety which inhabits most of the Western Isles. It has always lived and worked with the Scottish crofters and was used in farming, forestry, haulage and general riding, where its equable temperament and sure-footedness were valuable assets. It was also taken to war, used in both the Boer Wars and the First World War.

Even though there has been a stud book for the Highland Pony since the 1880s, no set breed standard exists; consequently, there is a diversity of types and bloodlines. Nevertheless, white marks are frowned upon and stallions with anything other than small stars on their foreheads cannot be registered. The Highland has proved equally popular in other countries, and there are studs in Europe, Australia, the United States and Canada.

The advent of pony-trekking in the 1950s made the Highland even more popular; this was not only because of its temperament, sturdiness and agility, but also because it could carry up to 210lb (95kg) with ease, making it suitable for both adults and children. Today the Highland is used in a number of children's riding events, including jumping, cross-country and pony club games, as well as in long-distance endurance events, showing and driving.

The Highland is a stocky, well-built pony. It has a small, pretty head, with a straight nose, small, often pricked ears, and large kind eyes. It has a strong body with a fairly long, well-developed neck, a neat shoulder, deep girth, and a well-muscled back. The legs are well-boned and sturdy, with hard, shapely hooves and feathering around the fetlocks. The mane and tail are thick and silky and are left long.

Highlands are friendly, with an even temperament and a willingness to work. They are hardy creatures, and although they require a little extra feeding, they are capable of living out in all types of weather.

They come in all solid colors, including gray and a variety of shades of fox, cream, gold, yellow and mouse. They can attain a height of up to 14.2hh.

BELOW & OPPOSITE: The Highland is a native Scottish breed and one of the largest of the mountain and moorland ponies of the British Isles.

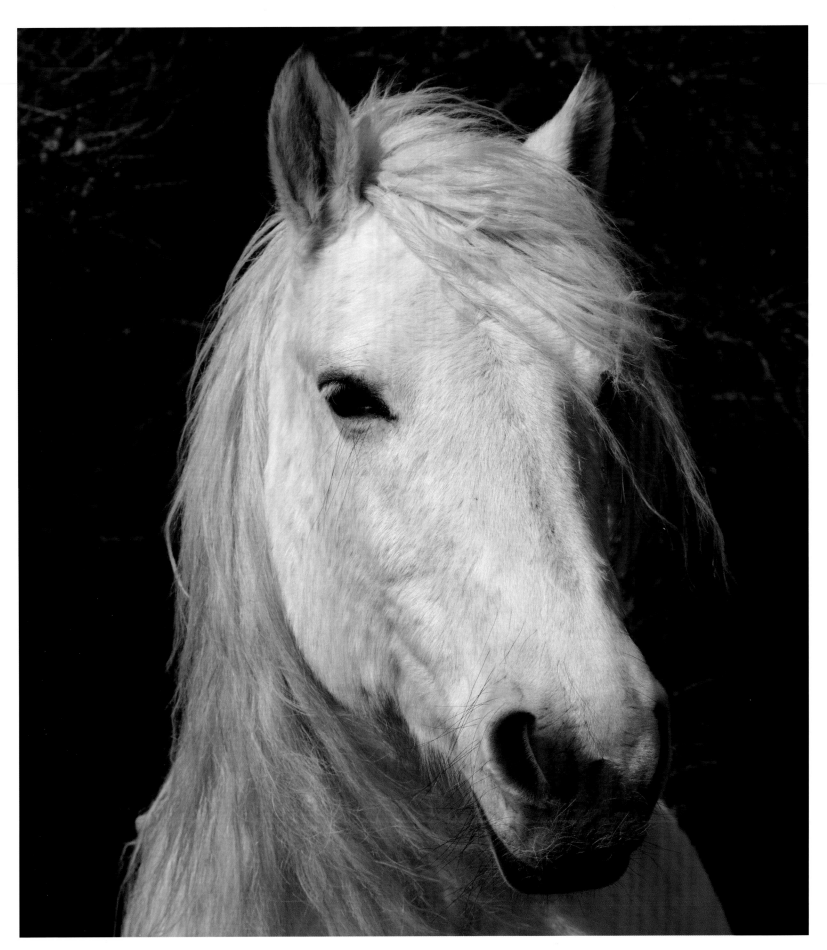

HOLSTEIN

The German Holstein, or Holsteiner, is probably descended from a native breed known as the Marsh Horse, which once roamed the wetlands of the Elbe estuary in what is now Schleswig-Holstein. The Holstein breed dates to the 13th century, when Gerhard I, Count of Holstein and Storman, permitted the monks of the Uetersen monastery to graze their quality horses, which they bred themselves, on private land. These were native stock that had been mixed with Andalusian, Neapolitan and Oriental blood to produce a heavy, useful horse. This was valued by farmers for its strength and reliability, and as a military horse for its courage, stamina and ability. It was also favored as a coaching horse. After the Reformation, the monastery land was returned to the landowners who continued the horse-breeding tradition.

By 1686 the Holstein had become so respected that strict guidelines were introduced to protect and improve the breed, which was by now popular throughout Europe. By the 18th century the Holstein's reputation had become so great that vast numbers of horses were exported. Unfortunately, not all of them had been bred to the exacting standards that had once prevailed and general deterioration set in.

By the 19th century, fortunately, the decline had been halted, and measures were now being taken to save and improve the breed. As

BELOW & OPPOSITE: The quality of Holstein breeding stock is ensured through annual inspections, when horses are evaluated and graded according to quality and to their potential for adding to the breeding pool.

the demand for warhorses grew less, the Holstein came to be used as a quality carriage horse, and to this end, Yorkshire Coach Horses and Cleveland Bay stallions were mated with Holstein mares. This was a great success, and the breed was given a new lease of life.

Thoroughbred was also added to refine the breed after the Second World War, which also improved the Holstein's jumping ability and general character. Today, it is a supreme sporthorse, excelling at dressage, showjumping and eventing. It has also been bred to good effect with other warmblood breeds, most effectively with the Hanoverian.

The Holstein is quite different from other warmbloods in that it has a large, rangy build resulting in a huge stride. The head is long and straight with large, flaring nostrils. The ears are expressive and the eyes are large and gentle. The long neck is elegant and well-developed, with high withers; the back is long and straight. The shoulders are shapely and sloping, which also contributes to its long stride. The chest is broad, the girth is deep, and the quarters are slightly sloping, muscular and powerful. The legs are long and muscular.

The Holstein is a fine, well-balanced horse, with an amazing ground-covering, elastic stride. The overall effect is of an elegant horse that carries itself lightly. It is good-natured, obedient and eager to work. Its large size and scope means that it is much in demand as a top-flight competition horse.

Holsteins are most commonly bay, though all solid colors, together with gray, are permitted. They stand around 16–17hh.

ABOVE & RIGHT: The Holstein is greatly respected as a competition horse, excelling at dressage, showjumping and eventing.

ICELANDIC

Iceland does not have its own indigenous breed of horse. What is known as the Icelandic Horse is derived from the Fjord and Døle horses of Norway, and the Celtics, Shetlands, Highlands and Connemaras of the British Isles, which were brought to Iceland by Scandinavian settlers in the 9th century. Because of the limited space on board their ships, the invaders would have brought only the best specimens, and once settled, would have allowed their horses to mate freely, producing the Icelandic breed as we know it today. This resulted in a hardy animal, able to tolerate semi-wild conditions and to survive harsh Arctic winters. It was used mainly for farming and for riding over icy terrain.

The Icelandic has been bred in closed pedigrees since the Middle Ages, because it must be traceable back to its Icelandic ancestors. Even though it is a pony in stature, it is always referred to as a horse; this is because there is no word for pony in the Icelandic language. It is often mentioned in the Icelandic Sagas, where to a warrior, a good horse was worth more than gold. Great horses were treated with respect and slain warriors would often have been buried alongside their mounts.

Icelandics have lately been exported to other countries, however, where cross-breeding has been allowed to take place.

This is a well-constructed animal. The head is of medium length, having a typical pony character with small pricked ears and soft,

BELOW & OPPOSITE: Icelandic horses are usually given names that reflect their color, temperament or other personal traits, often taken from Norse mythology. An example of this would be Grána, meaning "gray mare," and other Icelandic names might mean "happy one" or "the one with frost in his mane."

expressive eyes. The neck is well-set, and the chest is broad with a deep girth. The body and legs are stocky and strong and the feet are extremely hard.

The Icelandic is ideal for children, being tough, hardy and happy to live out all-year-round. It has two extra gaits: the *tølt*, which is a running walk with four beats, and is as fast as a canter and very comfortable; and the flying pace, which has two beats and is used for racing but which makes great demands on horse and rider. Speeds of up to 30mph (48km/h) can be reached using the flying pace, and to witness this is impressive indeed. The Icelandic is late to mature, however, and should not be backed until it is four years old. It can live to a ripe old age, often working up until 30; in fact, an Icelandic in Britain is known to have died aged 42.

Icelandics come in all solid colors as well as skewbald, palomino, dun and gray. A silver dapple coat is much prized; this is where the body is a rich brown and the mane and tail appear almost silver by contrast. In winter the coat is very thick, with three distinct layers. Icelandics stand between 12 and 13.2hh, and have been known to reach 14.2hh.

LEFT & BELOW: The Icelandic evolved from ponies brought to Iceland by Scandinavian settlers in the 9th century. They are referred to as horses, there being no word for pony in the Icelandic language.

KLADRUBER

The breed was established in 1597 by the Emperor Maximilian II of Austria, where it was bred at the Kladruber Stud which is situated in the former Czechoslovakia. Today the stud still produces Kladruber horses which are a mix of many different breeds. Heavy Alpine mares were originally mated with Barb and Turkish stallions, then later with Andalusian, Neapolitan and Lipizzaner, resulting in horses that were used exclusively to draw coaches and appear in parades of the Austrian Court in Vienna.

But the Second World War eventually took its toll of the breed with numbers plummeting to dangerously low levels; it was therefore decided to revive and improve the breed by adding Anglo-Norman, Hanoverian and Oldenburg bloodlines, which were mixed with the remaining stock. Today, the Kladruber is doing well and is used for general riding and for light haulage.

The Kladruber has inherited many of the attributes of the Andalusian, Neapolitan and Lipizzaner. The head is noble with a broad forehead, straight or slightly Roman nose, medium well-shaped ears, and an alert expression with large, kind and intelligent eyes. The neck is high-set and well-developed; the girth is deep and the chest broad. The body is of medium length and is sturdy with large quarters. The legs are well-muscled with good bone and well-shaped hooves.

The Kladruber has an equable temperament and is a willing and obedient worker. It has an attractive high-stepping action.

They are usually gray in color, though blacks are also bred. Height is 16.2–17hh.

BELOW & OPPOSITE: The Kladruber is impressive and proud. It is an amalgam of many breeds, including Andalusian, Neapolitan and Lipizzaner.

KNABSTRUP

The Knabstrup's origins go back 200 years or so, but its ancestry can be traced back even further, possibly to prehistoric Iberian horses. The Knabstrup is unusual for a European horse in that it has a distinctive spotted coat. This is thought to have been inherited from its prehistoric forebears, many of which can be seen depicted in primitive cave paintings.

Spotted horses were very popular at the courts of European royalty in the 16th and 17th centuries; but the Knabstrup was founded much later, in the early 1800s, when an Iberian mare of the Knabstrup Estate in Denmark was mated with a palomino Frederiksborg stallion. The foal was born with a spotted coat of many colors, which also had an attractive sheen. This horse became the foundation stallion of the Knabstrup breed.

OPPOSITE & BELOW: The Knabstrup's most distinctive feature is its spotted coat, which added to its popularity as a circus performer. Nowadays, its role is more often that of a general riding horse.

Unfortunately, because subsequent horses were bred primarily for their unusual coats, insufficient care and attention was given to their conformation, leading to gradual deterioration when the breed subsequently lost its popularity and almost disappeared. The horse has been improved in recent years, however, and the addition of Thoroughbred bloodlines has made it popular once more. Today it is used as a general riding horse and also features in showing classes and even circuses, due to its spotted coat.

The head is large, with a straight or Roman nose. The ears are small and well-pricked and the eyes have a kind, gentle expression. The muzzle is square, with large, open nostrils. The neck is high-set, the shoulders are well-developed, and the chest is broad. The back is rather long, with slightly sloping quarters, and the legs are strong with plenty of good bone. The mane and tail are rather sparse.

With its excellent natural paces, the Knabstrup is a good-quality riding horse. It is complaisant and intelligent, easy to train, and is an obedient and willing worker.

Colors and patterns are various, with permutations similar to those present in the Appaloosa. Full leopard spotting is the most highly prized, though one overall color or roan is also possible. Height is 15.2hh.

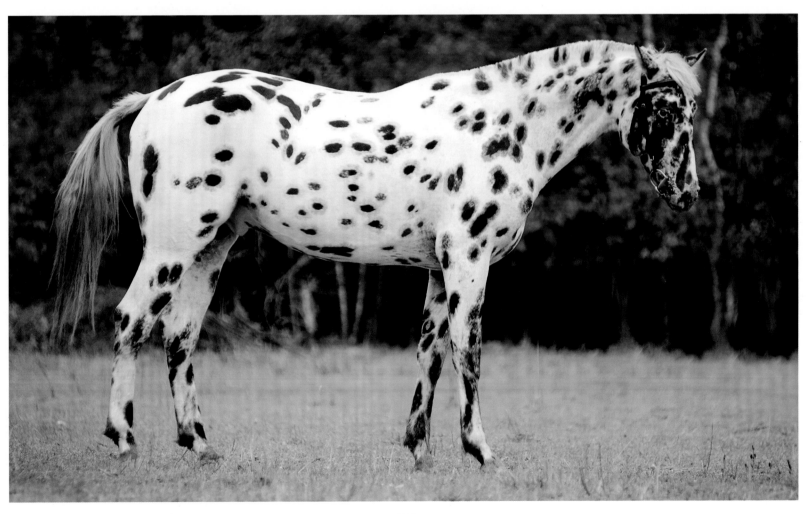

LIPIZZANER

The Lipizzaner is probably one of the world's most recognizable breeds due to its association with the Spanish Riding School of Vienna. Despite its origins in what is now Slovenia, the Lipizzaner has a far more ancient history, dating back to the 8th century and the Moorish occupation of Spain. The Moors brought horses of Oriental origin to Spain, such as Arabs and Barbs. These were bred with the heavier Iberian horses, which in turn produced the Andalusian – the most important element in the Lipizzaner's line of heredity.

In 1580 Archduke Charles, son of the Holy Roman Emperor Ferdinand I, who had inherited Austria-Hungary, sought to improve his horses, and decided on the system of haute école, or the practice

of advanced classical dressage. He founded a stud at Lipizza for the purpose, which also specialized in breeding carriage horses, and filled it with quality Spanish (Iberian) horses, known to be capable of the discipline. He used these horses as the foundation stock of the Lipizzaner, crossing them with heavier native breeds, together with Barb, Arab, Andalusian, Neapolitan and Kladruber. Thus, over a period of several hundred years, the classic riding horse was born.

The illustrious Spanish Riding School had been founded in Vienna in 1572. It got its name, not because of its Spanish riding

LEFT, ABOVE & OPPOSITE: Only Lipizzaner stallions are used for haute école in the Spanish Riding School of Vienna.

LUSITANO

The Lusitano shares its heritage with the Andalusian, both having been descended from the Iberian riding horse. The Lusitano gets its name (adopted only in the early 20th century) from Lusitania, which was the Roman name for Portugal. The origins of the breed date to around 25,000 BC and to the ancient ancestors of the Sorraia pony, which can be seen in cave paintings throughout the Iberian Peninsula.

Unlike the Andalusian, the Lusitano's breeding has remained truer to its Sorraia ancestry, in that it has only received infusions of Oriental, Garrano and Spanish blood. To keep the breed true to type, this mix hasn't been changed for centuries and care is taken to use only horses with obvious Iberian characteristics.

The Lusitano was bred mainly for agricultural use around the fertile River Tagus, where it is still used for the purpose. It is also used in bullfighting, as well as in haute école. Thankfully, in Portugal, the bull is not killed, and the entire business takes place with the rider on

LEFT & BELOW: The Portuguese Lusitano shares much of its ancestry with the Spanish Andalusian.

the horse's back. However, the Lusitano has to be incredibly agile and fast to avoid injury.

These horses are highly prized and receive haute école training to enhance their precision so that they can survive the demanding and dangerous spectacle. The Lusitano stallions are trained to these high standards before they are sent to stud, and all fighting horses are left entire; it is believed that geldings lack the courage and intelligence to work in the bullring.

Today, the horse is also used in lower levels of dressage. Infusions of Lusitano are also used to improve other breeds.

The Lusitano has a fine, noble countenance. The head is quite long, with a straight or slightly Roman nose and flared nostrils. The ears are of medium length, well-shaped and alert. The eyes are keen and intelligent, the neck is set high, with a well-developed muscular crest and well-defined withers. The sloping shoulders are powerful and the chest is broad with a deep girth. The back is short

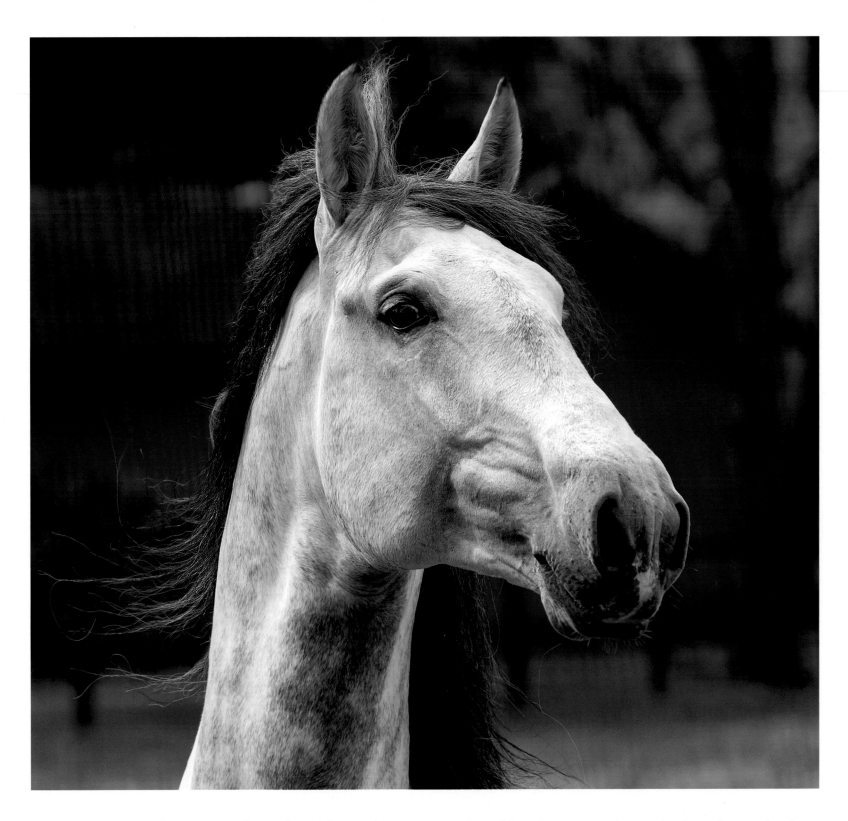

OPPOSITE & ABOVE: The Lusitano makes a talented dressage horse, having a natural high-stepping action that is most attractive.

and strong and the loins broad, with quarters that are not too large. The Lusitano's high-stepping action is attributed to its strong, long hocks, which are capable of great impulsion, and the deep flexion is achieved by a well-developed second thigh (stifle).

This noble and courageous horse is kind, good-natured and obedient. It is level-headed and not given to sudden panic, which are important attributes in a fighting horse. Lusitanos have competed in several Olympics and World Equestrian Games as part of the Portuguese and Spanish dressage teams.

They may be any solid color as well as gray, and they stand between 15 and 16hh.

NEW FOREST

The New Forest Pony is probably a descendant of the Celtic Pony, as are all the British native breeds, though the earliest mention of it was in the time of King Canute (c.995–1035), famous for ordering back the sea's incoming tide.

The New Forest is in the county of Hampshire in southern England and consists mainly of scrubland, bog and moorland, which has led to the development of a hardy animal, designed to survive harsh conditions. Over the years, Thoroughbred and Arab blood were introduced, mainly to increase size and performance and to improve the pony's appearance, but is was not until the end of the

THESE PAGES & OVERLEAF: New Forests are hardy ponies that will happily live in the wild, and ponies such as these have been grazing the common land of the New Forest for many hundreds of years.

19th century, during the reign of Queen Victoria, that a structured breeding program was initiated. At the same time, other British breeds were also introduced, such as Dartmoor, Exmoor, Welsh, Fell, Dales and Highland ponies.

In 1891, the Society for the Improvement of New Forest Ponies was founded to ensure that there was an ample supply of quality stallions living in the New Forest and this, in turn, led to the official publication of the first stud book in 1910. Nowadays, although still living and breeding in their home environment, many quality ponies are also bred in private studs all over the world.

The New Forest Pony is one of the larger breeds native to Britain. It is an ideal child's or teenager's pony and excellent for driving. It has a well-proportioned body that is more slender than other British breeds, and well-formed feet.

The ponies are calm, good-natured and a pleasure to own – substantial enough for dressage, showjumping and cross-country; in fact, it is often said that a good New Forest Pony can rise to any occasion.

Coats can be any color, with touches of white, while height is in the range of 12–14.2hh.

OLDENBURG

Bred originally as a coach horse, the Oldenburg is the heaviest of the modern German warmbloods. It dates from the early part of the 17th century, when Count Anton Guenther initiated a program for the breed.

The Oldenburg's earliest ancestors were heavy Friesian horses that were infused with Spanish and Arabian bloodlines. The breed was stabilized in the 19th century by introduction of Thoroughbred, Cleveland Bay, Yorkshire Coach Horse, Anglo-Norman and Hanoverian bloodlines.

The Oldenburg was also used by the military as a strong artillery horse. As the years passed, however, the need for such horses began to diminish. It was replaced by a demand for a lighter riding horse, suitable for pleasure and competition.

In the second half of the 20th century, bloodlines of lighter horses were again introduced, such as Thoroughbred, Trakehner, Hanoverian and Westphalian. Nowadays, the Oldenburg excels at dressage and showjumping; it retains its ability as a coach or carriage horse, however, and is used for the purpose to this day.

The Oldenburg is distinguished by its noble head and proud, workmanlike air. It has a high-set neck, long shoulder, strong back, and a well-muscled croup with strong joints. It can be used not only as an elegant dressage horse, but also as a powerful showjumper, having a large frame and a long, active stride.

The Oldenburg resembles a hunter type. Its character is equable, making it pleasant to handle and ride. It is usually black, bay or brown, and stands between 16.2 and 17.2hh.

BELOW & OPPOSITE: From humble beginnings as a coach horse, the Oldenburg has evolved into a very capable modern sporthorse.

SHETLAND

The Shetlands consist of 100 or so offshore islands lying off the north-eastern coast of Scotland. The islands are remote and have a harsh climate, particularly in winter, and there is not much shelter for the ponies that inhabit them. Food is scarce, but the ponies have adapted to survive on very little. They live on next to nothing during the winter months, but it is known that they come down from the hills to feed on the seaweed that has been washed up on the beaches.

It is unclear where these ponies originated, but there is evidence from Bronze Age remains that they have been present for a very long time, probably descended from the Celtic Pony. Alternatively, they may have crossed the ice from Scandinavia, or may even have come from Europe.

Traditionally, Shetlands were used by islanders as riding, plowing, pack and harness ponies. In 1870, the Londonderry Stud at Bressay, Scotland, fixed the type and character of the breed and today's best stock can still be traced to the famous Londonderry sires, even though the stud no longer exists.

OPPOSITE & BELOW: Shetland Ponies have been living on Shetland for at least 2,500 years, where the harsh climate and scarcity of food have developed them into the hardy animals that exist today.

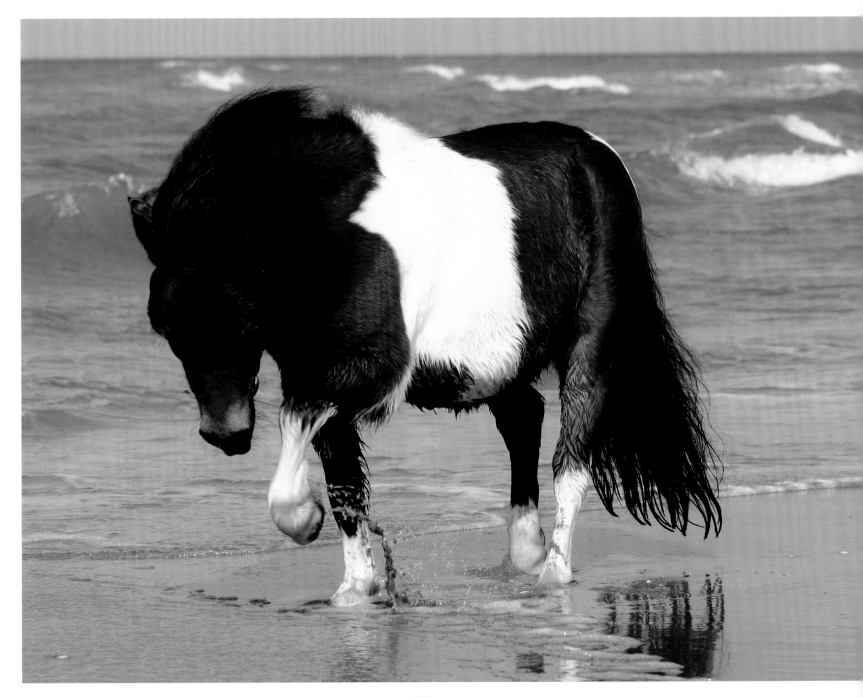

The Shetland's head is small and neat and can be slightly dished. The ears are small and the eyes open and bold. The neck, shoulders and withers are well-defined; the chest and quarters must be strong and muscular. The mane and tail is profuse, with straight feathering on the legs. The coat is double-layered – a feature unique to the Shetland Pony.

The Shetland has plenty of character and can be willful on occasions. Because it is relatively strong for its size, unless it has been properly trained and has good manners, it may be too much for a small child. But when kept in a suitable environment, with adult help on hand, Shetlands make superb children's ponies.

Shetlands can be most colors, and black, brown, bay, chestnut, gray, piebald and skewbald are all common.

Standard Shetlands grow to a maximum height of 42in (107cm). Since the 1980s, however, a miniature Shetland has been developed which does not exceed 34in (86cm).

BELOW & OPPOSITE: The Shetland is possibly the most famous of the small breeds.

THOROUGHBRED

The Thoroughbred is probably the most important breed of all and is the best known of all the British breeds. Its history dates to the 17th century, when English farmers and landowners became increasingly interested in racing. Until that time, local horses, not having been specifically bred for the purpose, were being raced, and it soon became apparent that a selective breeding program was required to make them more suitable for the task. This became more urgent as gambling became popular with the public at large.

The wealthier landowners realized that while the native horses had stamina, they were lacking in speed, so between 1689 and 1729, in order to improve the stock, they began to import horses

ABOVE & OPPOSITE: All Thoroughbreds registered in the General Stud Book, opened in 1791, can trace their pedigree back to the three Arabian foundation sires. Currently, Thoroughbreds are raced in over 50 countries of the world.

from the Middle East. It is generally accepted that the modern Thoroughbred stems from three such stallions: the Byerley Turk, the Darley Arabian and the Godolphin Arabian, all of which had a long experience of working at stud. Between them, they established the three bloodlines of Herod, Eclipse and Matchem, which were pivotal to the British Thoroughbred – a name not applied to the breed until 1821.

Although initially bred with racing in mind, the qualities of the Thoroughbred make it an ideal horse for all other equestrian disciplines, e.g. eventing, showjumping, dressage, etc. Not only has the Thoroughbred been exported far and wide to improve racing stocks, it has also been used to improve hundreds of other breeds around the world.

Descendants of the three foundation sires reached the United States in the 1730s, where they were generally similar to Thoroughbreds elsewhere; recently, however, a distinctive American type has emerged, with longer hindlegs and a longer stride, making its quarters appear higher in comparison.

The Thoroughbred is a beautiful and athletic animal, with long, clean limbs, a fine, silky coat, an elegant profile and a muscular body. The eyes are always large and intelligent and the ears finely sculpted. Built for toughness, stamina and speed, the Thoroughbred is regarded as the ultimate racing machine.

Thoroughbreds are courageous, honest and bold, and one only has to be present at a steeplechase or hurdle race to see that this is so. The Thoroughbred is often described as "hot-headed," and while this may be true of some individuals, which are more sensitive than others, most are a pleasure to own and ride.

Pure-bred and Thoroughbred are not synonymous in this context: the latter, in this case, is the actual name of this breed.

All true colors are acceptable, and height is usually between 15 and 16.2hh.

LEFT: The classically bred Thoroughbred is not only beautiful to behold but also has great speed and stamina. It is the king of the horse world, and as a performer is second to none. Its bloodlines have improved many other breeds, particularly the warmbloods.

TRAKEHNER

The Trakehner is the most elegant of the warmbloods and is the nearest in character to the Thoroughbred. Nowadays, because of its athleticism and paces, it is predominantly used for competition, particularly dressage and eventing.

The Trakehner has had a checkered history dating to 1732, when the first Trakehner stud was founded in East Prussia, part of the former kingdom of Prussia and now in Poland. The stud became the main source of stallions for the whole of Prussia and the area quickly became famous for its beautiful and elegant coach horses.

THESE PAGES & OVERLEAF: The Trakehner is the purest of the warmblood breeds; this is because it has a closed stud book.

HORSES OF WESTERN EUROPE

The breed came into being when native horses of the region were bred with Thoroughbreds and Arabs, infusions which gave the Trakehner its speed and endurance. Within 50 years, however, the emphasis had shifted from producing coach horses to breeding chargers for the cavalry, which continued until the Second World War, when the Trakehner stud was completely destroyed. Fortunately, toward the end of the war, about 1,000 horses were saved when they were trekked west, accompanied by refugees escaping from the Russian invasion. Although some of the horses died on the way, due to the harsh conditions, sufficient survived to continue the breed. Today, the breeding of the Trakehner is again flourishing in its place of origin as well as in other countries.

In terms of appearance, the Trakehner resembles the middleweight Thoroughbred. The head is fine, with an intelligent and interested expression. The profile is straight and similar to that of the Thoroughbred. The neck and shoulders are shapely, the back short and strong and the quarters powerful. The legs are strong and straight, producing a powerful, straight action.

The Trakehner has an excellent temperament, being amiable, obedient and courageous. Although it resembles the Thoroughbred, it is without the "hot" temperament associated with that breed. For this reason, breeders looking for an infusion of Thoroughbred without this trait often select Trakehner stallions instead. All solid colors are acceptable and height is usually around 16–16.2hh.

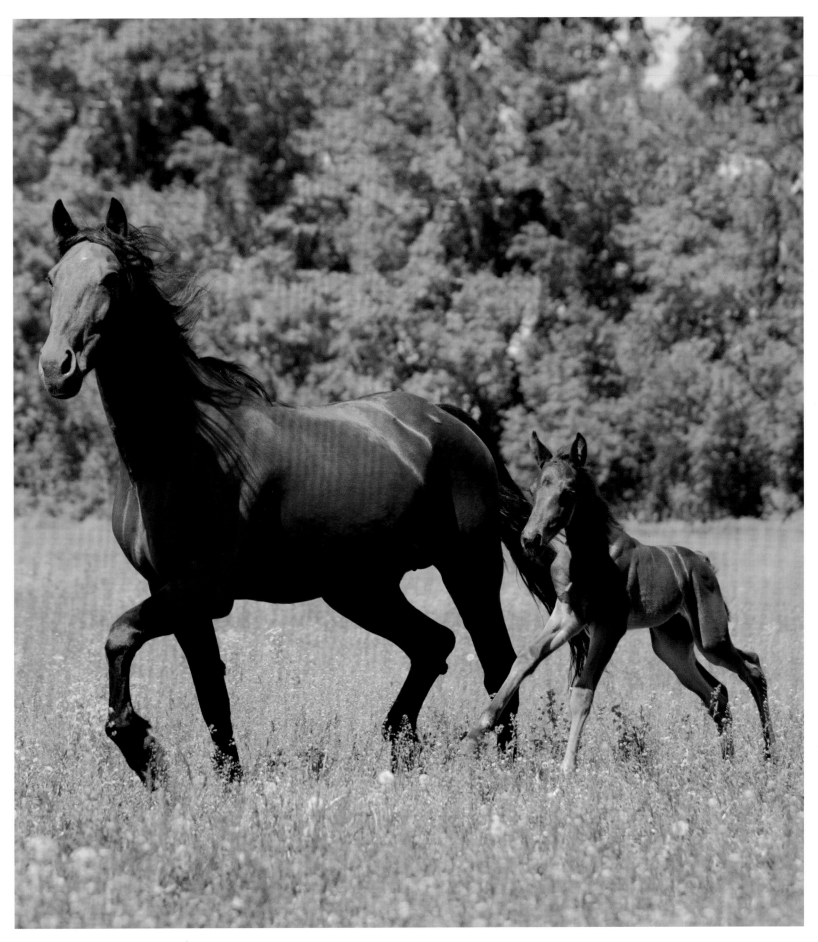

WARMBLOOD

Today the warmblood, is considered to be the ultimate modern competition horse, and almost every country in the world has its own variation.

Warmbloods are calmer creatures, having a heavier build than hotbloods. They have been bred for their extravagant paces and biddable natures, making them excellent performers at jumping and dressage. They are the result of interbreeding with heavier coldbloods such as Shires and Cleveland Bays and were originally bred as warhorses and for lighter work on farms, mainly in northern Europe.

Today, competition warmbloods are generally bred on stud farms, where each horse is carefully selected for its abilities. Some bloodlines result in the breeding of valuable and famous dressage horses, while

BELOW & OPPOSITE: Warmbloods have been bred in a variety of colors, some of which are featured here.

others produce the fabulous, careful showjumpers. Many of the young horses are "performance tested" so that only the very best go on to breed. Examples are Hanoverian, Dutch Warmblood, Selle Français, American Warmblood, Holstein, Danish Warmblood, British Warmblood and Belgian Warmblood.

All the warmblood breeds are extremely beautiful with plenty of presence and substance in their movement. Whichever the origin all are a delight to ride as well as own.

OPPOSITE: The Danish Warmblood was established in the 20th century as a superb quality horse. It excels as a sporthorse, particularly in dressage and showjumping.

BELOW: Bred to be a cavalry horse, the Swedish Warmblood is now used mainly as a quality competition horse.

OPPOSITE: The Belgian Warmblood was created as a sporthorse and is a regular participant in top competition, particularly dressage and showjumping. Those that don't quite make the grade, however, make fine riding horses.

BELOW & OVERLEAF: The Dutch Warmblood is probably the most celebrated of the warmblood sporthorses. It continues to excel in competition year after year.

THE WELSH BREEDS

Horses were present in Wales as much as 10,000 years ago. At that time, the indigenous breed inhabiting the hills was the Celtic Pony, and it is thought that all Welsh ponies known today derive from this ancient breed.

It is recorded that native stock was being bred in Wales in around 50 BC, when Julius Caesar founded a stud in Merionethshire and was responsible for introducing Arab blood into the breed. The first mention of Welsh ponies and cobs appears in the laws of Hywel Dda, written in AD 930.

Throughout the centuries, variations on the original wild ponies were developed. Early on in the 20th century, the Welsh Pony and Cob Society identified the four clear types. These are the original, once wild, Welsh Mountain Pony not exceeding 12hh (Section A); the Welsh Pony not exceeding 13hh (Section B); the Welsh Pony of Cob Type up to 13.2hh (Section C); the Welsh Cob of 13.2–15.2hh (Section D).

The Welsh Mountain Pony (Section A) is the oldest of all the Welsh breeds. As the name suggests it is tough, resilient, sound in limb as well as constitution. Known for its intelligence, agility, endurance and hardiness, the Welsh Mountain Pony is capable of surviving the harshest of winters. These ponies are now found all over

BELOW & OPPOSITE: The Welsh Mountain Pony (Section A) is the oldest of the Welsh breeds.

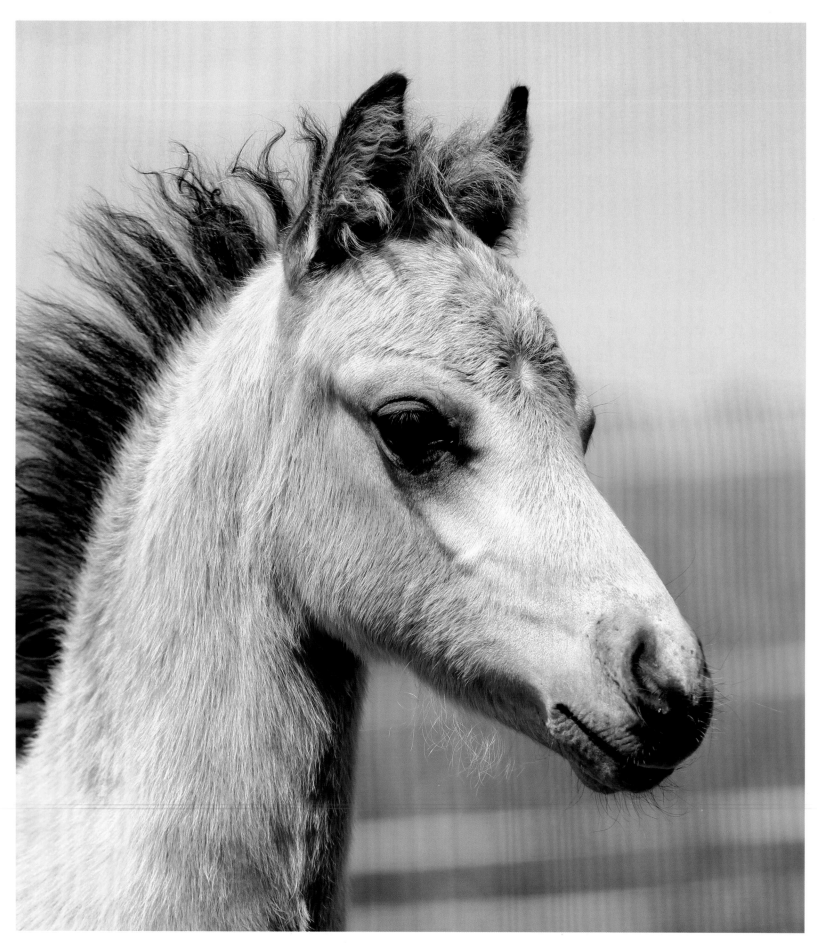

the world and are highly regarded as quality children's riding ponies; they also perform well in harness.

The head is refined, with a slim tapering muzzle and small, pricked ears. The eyes are large and bold. These qualities, as well as a dished face, give the Welsh Mountain a distinct resemblance to the Arab, a breed that has been introduced. The neck, well-defined

OPPOSITE & BELOW: The Welsh (Section B) is rather more refined in looks than the Welsh Mountain. It is used for showing and makes an excellent riding pony for children.

withers and quarters are in proportion to the rest of the pony's body, while the tail is set quite high. The limbs are set square, with well-made joints, and the feet are small, rounded and hard.

The Welsh Mountain has great personality and charm, having inherited intelligence and quick-wittedness – traits which the original wild ponies seemed to have possessed in abundance. When in action, the gaits should be smooth and the hocks well-flexed. They are usually gray, but all true colors are acceptable.

The Welsh Pony (Section B) has all the best attributes of the Welsh Mountain Pony, though breeders have accentuated its

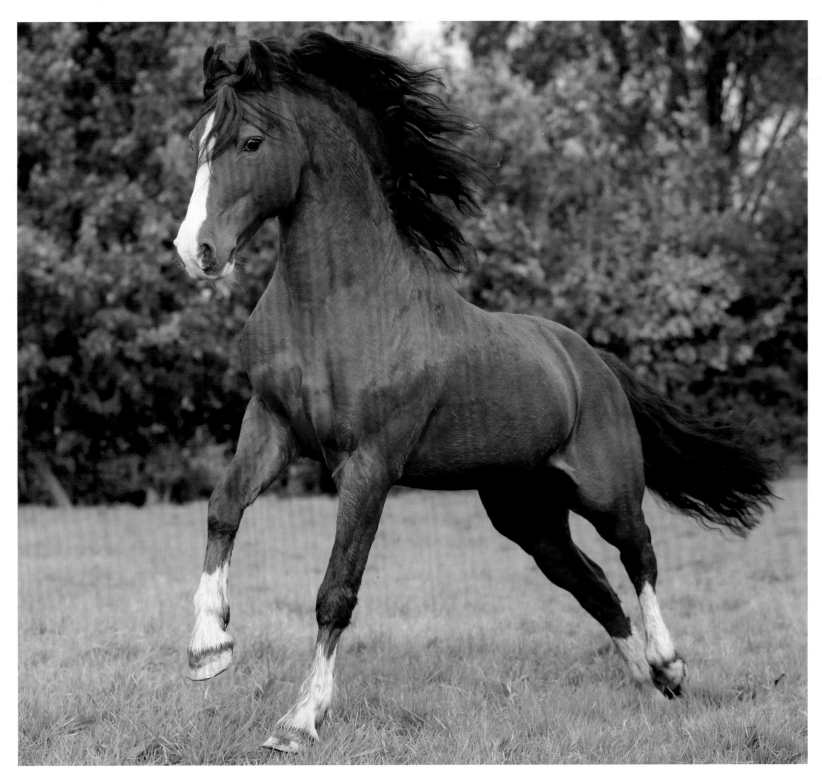

talents as a riding pony. Moreover, because the Welsh Pony has been used for generations on farms for herding sheep, it has similar toughness and agility.

These qualities, when combined with good looks, jumping ability, and superb conformation for riding, makes them perfect as children's mounts.

The Welsh Pony shares many similarities with the Welsh Mountain Pony. The head is refined, with small pricked ears, and the face may be slightly dished. The eyes are large and intelligent. The neck, back and quarters are muscular and in proportion, and the tail is set high. The limbs are straight and strong and the hooves strong and rounded.

OPPOSITE & ABOVE: The Welsh Pony of Cob Type (Section C) resembles a small cob and is a little larger than Section A and B examples.

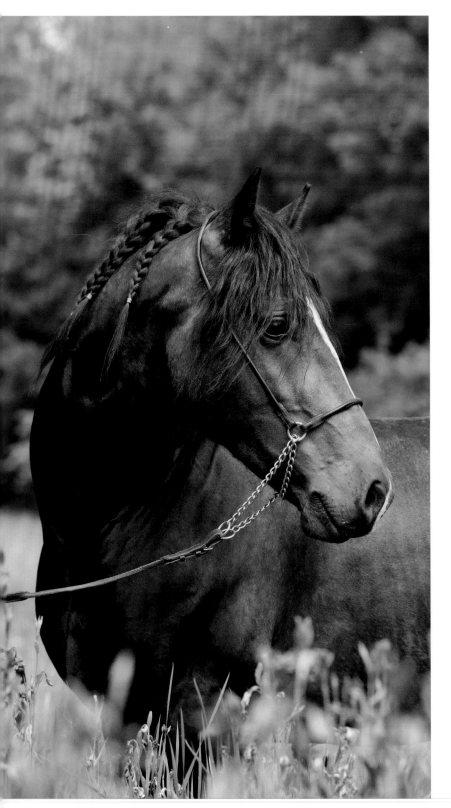

heavier loads. It was developed more as a harness pony than for ridden work and has a naturally pronounced action, probably inherited from the Hackney, which was introduced into the breed.

General appearance is of a small cob. The eyes are spaced widely apart and the expression is intelligent. Like the others, the ears are small and pricked. The body and legs are sturdier and more cob-like than those of the Welsh Pony, and the feet are slightly larger. Mane and tail are full.

The Welsh Pony of Cob Type is similar in temperament to the other Welsh breeds, being lively and enthusiastic. It performs well in harness and is also a natural jumper.

All true colors are acceptable, but for the show ring, ponies are preferred with plenty of white on the lower legs.

Of all the Welsh breeds, the Welsh Cob (Section D) is the most famous. Known for its handsome appearance and extravagant paces, not only is it the ultimate working cob, it is also guaranteed to command attention in the show ring.

The breed dates from the 11th century, when it was known as the Powys Cob or Powys Rouncy. Welsh Cobs not only possess Welsh Mountain Pony blood, they were also influenced by imports from all over the Roman Empire. Breeds from Spain, such as the Andalusian, and the Barb and Arab from North Africa, were all crossed with the early Welsh Cob variety. Later in the 18th and 19th centuries other breeds, such as Hackney and Yorkshire Coach Horse, were also introduced.

Welsh Cobs were traditionally used by the military as well as by farmers, but they were so versatile that they could be used by virtually anyone needing transport or light haulage.

The Welsh Cob is compact, well-muscled, well-balanced and strong. It has a fine head with large, intelligent eyes and the usual small, pricked ears. The neck is arched and muscular, the back is short-coupled for strength, and the quarters are powerful and rounded. The legs are sturdy and straight and the hard and rounded feet are in proportion with the animal's body.

The Welsh Cob is proud, courageous, and extravagant in action. It is suitable for all disciplines and for all riders.

All true colors are acceptable.

The Welsh Pony is willing, active and enthusiastic and will always give of its best. Like the Welsh Mountain they are predominantly gray, but all true colors are acceptable.

The Welsh Pony of Cob Type (Section C) was originally used for farm work – also for carting slate from the mines. It is of a similar height to the Welsh Pony, but sturdier and capable of carrying

LEFT & OPPOSITE: The Welsh Cob (Section D) is also very cobby in appearance. It is larger than the other three types and is the most striking in appearance with extravagant paces. Its size means that it can be comfortably ridden by the entire family.

WESTPHALIAN

Like most European warmbloods, the Westphalian is based on an older, heavier breed which had been native to Westphalia for hundreds of years. This native coldblood was crossed with Thoroughbred to produce a warmblood, which was first registered as a Westphalian in 1826, when the stud book was opened.

For many years, the horse was used for riding and light carriage work until measures were taken to improve the breed at the end of the Second World War. To improve its speed and endurance, as well as its intelligence, Westphalian stock was infused with more

A PASSION FOR HORSES

Thoroughbred and Arab blood, while Hanoverian was also added to ensure good sense and obedience.

The result was a riding horse of superb quality which received its true recognition as a competition horse, particularly in showjumping, in the 1970s. Nowadays it not only excels at dressage but also at eventing.

OPPOSITE LEFT & RIGHT & BELOW: The Westphalian is a quality horse used for showjumping, dressage and eventing.

The head is handsome and broad, with medium- to wide-apart ears, a straight nose and clever eyes. The neck is long and well-developed, with fairly prominant withers, a straight back, strong loins and well-muscled quarters. The shoulders are sloping, with a broad chest and deep girth. The legs are well-porportioned and strong with plenty of bone.

The Westaphalian is well-known for its courage and spirit. It is also obedient and easy to handle.

All solid colors are permitted, with white on the lower legs and head. Height is between 15.2 and 16.2hh.

CHAPTER FOUR
HORSES OF EASTERN EUROPE

"At once the coursers from the barrier bound;
The lifted scourges all at once resound;
Loose on their shoulders the long manes reclined
Float in their speed, and dance upon the wind."

—Homer

BASHKIR CURLY

The Bashkir was once bred by the Bashkiri people, living in the southern Urals in the former U.S.S.R. They used the horses to pull their troikas, while the mares' milk was used to make kumiss, a fermented alcoholic drink. The breed is very old and has evolved in an extraordinary fashion. It has the stocky body, large head and small nostrils common to horses raised in cold climates; but the strangest feature is its winter coat, which grows to a length of 6 inches (15cm), falling into tight ringlets.

The Bashkir is known in the United States as the Bashkir Curly. Some have also been imported into the United Kingdom, where they are used mainly for showing and endurance riding. Back in their native land, however, they are used in harness and their long hair is spun into fabric; moreover, they are used for meat and their milk is still used. The Bashkir's blood is another strange factor, in that its composition is different from that of other horses; they also have higher respiratory and heart rates.

The original Bashkir had a large head with small ears. The eyes have an intelligent expression, the nose is straight, and the nostrils are small. The U.S. version has been bred with a smaller head, which appears to balance more neatly on the body. It has a well-developed neck, longish body, and the short stocky legs typical of horses from cold climates, where they develop a layer of fat in winter to keep themselves warm. Oddly enough, they shed out the mane hair (and sometimes even the tail) each summer, which grows back during winter. Foals arrive with thick, crinkly coats, curls inside their ears, and curly eyelashes.

Good-natured, affectionate and willing workers, Bashkirs are commonly chestnut, palomino or bay, and stand at about 14hh.

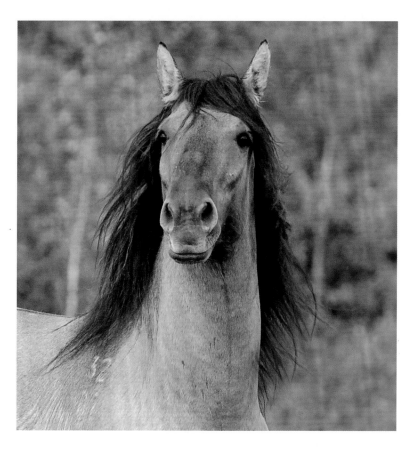

LEFT & ABOVE: The Bashkir has the wide-set eyes characteristic of Oriental breeds and said to provide it with a wider range of vision. It is a very old breed, well-adapted to cold conditions in that it grows a long, thick, curly coat to help it through the winter months.

DON

The Don is Russia's most famous breed. It originated in the harsh Russian steppes, where it once roamed in herds, surviving the freezing winters and torrid summers with nothing but sparse vegetation for food.

The original steppes breed, known as the Old Don, was bred with various Orientals, such as the Arab, Karabakh and Turkmene, and Orlov and Thoroughbred were added to improve its conformation and provide it with incredible stamina.

The horse was the preferred mount of the Don Cossacks; it was also used by the Russian army, and its extreme toughness made it particularly popular with wolf-hunters. Today, the Don's hardy constitution makes it an excellent endurance horse. It is also used to improve other breeds.

The overall picture of the Don is one of strength and robustness. The head is fairly small and neat, the slightly dished or straight nose clearly indicating its Arab heritage. Ears are small and shapely and the eyes are large and intelligent. The neck is set high and should be arched; however, many have ewe necks. The back is fairly long, straight and wide, with sloping quarters and a straight shoulder. The legs are clean but in some cases can be sickle-hocked. Moreover, the placement of the pelvis tends to restrict movement and causes a stilted action – a fault that has now been largely bred out. The hooves are well-shaped and hard.

Tough and sturdy, with an independent spirit, these qualities have found their way into other breeds. The most striking feature of the Don's coat is its iridescent sheen. It is most commonly chestnut, but can also be bay, brown, black and gray. It stands approximately 15.2hh.

THESE PAGES & OVERLEAF: The Don, the favorite mount of the Cossacks, originated in the harsh conditions of the Russian steppes; it is consequently hardy and able to withstand extremes of temperature.

KABARDIN

The Kabardin is descended from the Tarpan – the wild horse of Eastern Europe and Asia, which sadly became extinct in captivity in 1887. The Kabardin remained unchanged in type until the Russian Revolution when, like many other Russian horses, steps were taken to improve the breed. The original Kabardin was bred with Karabakh, Turkmene, Persian and Arab to create a much bigger, stronger horse, suitable for riding and general farm work, also for use as a packhorse. The Kabardin is also an excellent mountain horse – possibly the best there is – being sure-footed, agile and intelligent, with the innate ability to search out the safest routes. Its great stamina enables it to work all day without becoming stressed.

The breed remains popular in its place of origin to this day. This is now the Republic of Kabardino-Balkaria, where it is still used for light draft work and for riding. Elsewhere, it is used in competition and to improve other breeds.

The Karbardin has a longish head, often with a slightly Roman nose. The longish ears point inwards and are set close together. The eyes are wise and intelligent and the nostrils flared. The neck is long and well-developed, and the back is straight and strong; the legs are long and fine, but at the same time also very strong. The overall impression is of a horse with strong Oriental influences.

Kabardins are kind, obedient, intelligent and trustworthy. They are a hardy breed, and with extra feeding can live out all year. They have strong constitutions and mostly live to a ripe old age.

Colors may be bay, black, brown and very occasionally gray. Height is somewhere between 14.2 and 15.1hh.

THESE PAGES & OVERLEAF: The Kabardin is the principal breed of the Northern Caucasus and is used to improve native stock in Armenia, Azerbaijan and Georgia. The best Kabardins are raised at the Karachai and Malka studs, and crossings with Thoroughbreds are becoming popular.

ORLOV TROTTER

The Orlov, or Orloff, Trotter is one of the foremost breeds of its type in the world. It was founded in the 18th century by Count Alexey Orlov, whose ambition it was to produce a superb trotting horse. He founded a stud at Ostrov, near Moscow, for the purpose, bringing in a large number of Arab horses. One of these was the stallion Smetanka, a silver-gray horse, large and rather long-backed for the breed, with an extravagant trot. After a season, Orlov was left with a few progeny, bred from Dutch Harddraver, Mecklenburg, Danish, Thoroughbred and Arabian mares.

Orlov decided to look for a better stud farm, with more grazing, which he found in Khrenovoye in the Voronezh region to the south of Moscow. He considered it perfect for his purpose, in that there were vast areas of grassland, clear springs, and a dry climate.

The Khrenovoye Stud was thus founded in 1778, and the following year produced a colt called Polkan I, which in turn was mated with a Danish mare carrying Spanish blood. The result

LEFT, ABOVE & OPPOSITE: The Orlov Trotter is most famous for its impressive action. It is a well-bred, attractive horse and was once the toast of the 19th-century racing fraternity, although its popularity gradually declined due to the advent of faster breeds such as the French Trotter and Standardbred.

was a foal called Bars I, which eventually showed exceptional stamina and trotting abilities and became the foundation stallion of the Orlov breed.

The Orlov is a muscular horse, famous for its exceptional and impressive action. Its stamina and quality ensured that it reigned supreme on the race track until the end of the 19th century, when Standardbreds and later French Trotters were introduced to the scene. Unfortunately, the Orlov is now in crisis, which is largely due to the introduction of these faster breeds.

The Orlov has a small, elegant head, with a noble profile and ears highly reminiscent of those of the Arab horse. The hindquarters are powerful and, like many trotters, the shoulders are straight. It is energetic, sure-footed and bold. Owing to its swift, balanced trot, it is suitable for riding and driving as well as trotting.

Orlovs are usually gray, black or bay and range from 15.2–17hh in height.

BELOW & OPPOSITE: Leo Tolstoy, the author of War and Peace, *immortalized one such exceptional trotter in his novella,* Kholstomer (Strider): The Story of a Horse.

SHAGYA ARABIAN

The Shagya Arabian comes from Hungary's second most famous breeding establishment, the Babolna Stud, founded in the late 1700s; the other is the Mezöhegyes Stud.

In 1816 the military stipulated that all brood mares should be bred with Oriental stallions to provide cavalry and harness horses; stallions with mixed Oriental blood as well as Iberian crosses were also used. The results, although fairly lightweight, were horses that were tough and had a good deal of stamina.

Following this success, it was decided that the Bobolna Stud should concentrate on breeding horses with predominantly Arab blood, which was the beginning of the excellent Shagya Arabian.

Today's breed is descended from one Arab stallion, called Shagya, which was brought from Syria in 1836. He was fairly large for an Arab,

BELOW & OPPOSITE: The action of the Shagya, like that of all Arabians, is unique. It is free and elastic as though it were moving on springs.

standing at 15.2½hh, and was from the Siglavi or Seglawy strain. The stallion was typically Arab in conformation, with a fine dished nose, a proud high-crested neck, a short body, and a high-set tail. It was mated with the military-style mares to produce the first Shagya Arabians and subsequent breeding by selection has produced a beautiful, refined riding horse of the highest possible quality. Today Shagya Arabians make excellent riding and competition horses and are also used for driving. They remain popular in their native land, but are relatively rare elsewhere.

The Shagya is very like the Arab in conformation, but a little heavier. The head is wedge-shaped, with a wide forehead and a straight or dished nose. The ears are neatly pointed and alert, and the eyes are kind. The muzzle is small and delicate, with large flaring nostrils. The neck is beautifully arched, well-muscled, and set high.

The shoulders are sloping, with a broad chest and deep girth; the body is fairly short, with well-defined quarters and long, elegant legs; well-muscled at the top, the legs have more bone than those of the traditional Arab.

The Shagya has the constitution of the Arab but is bigger and stronger. It is kind, noble and spirited, and has great stamina, speed and agility.

All solid colors are acceptable, although many have inherited the Shagya stallion's gray color. Rarest of all is black. They stand somewhere between 14.2 and 15.2hh.

BELOW & OPPOSITE: Shagya Arabs stem from one stallion, Shagya, which was imported to Hungary from Syria in 1836.

TERSKY

The Tersky or Tersk is a true performance horse, specializing in endurance, racing, jumping and dressage. Not only has it excellent sporting and athletic capabilities, it is also one of the most beautiful of the Russian breeds.

Originating in the Northern Caucasus, the breed is now concentrated at the Stavropol Stud. Breeding and rearing previously took place on the steppes, with the result that weaker stock succumbed to wolves or died of disease. Learning to survive, therefore, made the breed tough.

The modern breed is a product of the early 20th century; it was based on the Strelets Arab, produced by crossing Anglo-Arabs with Orlovs, and was developed by crossing Arabs with old-type Terskys to which Thoroughbred blood had been also introduced.

There are three variations on the Tersky: the first is lightweight, fine and Arab-like in appearance, and is known as the Eastern type.

The second is middleweight, sturdier and longer in the back, with a frame that is thicker-set, while the third is the heavier type that has received infusions of Trakehner.

The Tersky is a horse of medium height and great beauty, which reflects its Arabian heritage. The head is finely formed with a dished profile; the eyes are large and intelligent and the nostrils flared.

The Tersky has an equable temperament that combines kindness and intelligence with courage and stamina.

They are predominantly gray, usually with a metallic sheen to the coat, while black, chestnut and bay are also possible. They stand between 15 and 16hh.

THESE PAGES & OVERLEAF: The Tersky is the ultimate sporthorse with all the stamina, grace and beauty of the Arab.

CHAPTER FIVE

HORSES OF ASIA

"The wind of heaven is that which blows between a horse's ears."

—Arabian Proverb

AKHAL-TEKE

The Akhal-Teke of Turkmenistan, a republic in central Asia lying between the Caspian Sea and Afghanistan, is believed to be a descendant of the Turkoman or Turkmene, an ancient race of horses thought to have existed thousands of years ago, but now unfortunately extinct. It takes its name from the Teke tribe, which still

BELOW & OPPOSITE: Horses such as these have incredible stamina. For example, in a test of endurance in 1935, 15 Akhal-Tekes traveled from Ashkhabad to Moscow on a march of approximately 2,600 miles (4185km), which also entailed crossing the 255-mile (410-km) Karakum Desert. The entire trip lasted for approximately 84 days.

inhabits the Akhal Oasis in the Karakum Desert, close to the border with Iran. Here the horses are traditionally kept in herds under the watchful eyes of mounted herdsmen. This aristocrat of the desert is long, slim elegance personified, but it also has a hardy constitution and can go for long periods without water. In their protected environment, however, the horses are well-tended by the herdsman, who use heavy rugs to cover their backs during extremes of heat and cold. They were once hand-fed a high-protein diet, which surprisingly included eggs and mutton fat.

Historically, this "heavenly" horse was prized by such warlords as Alexander the Great, Darius the Mede and Genghis Khan, while Marco Polo praised the Turkoman horse in his *Travels*. Nowadays,

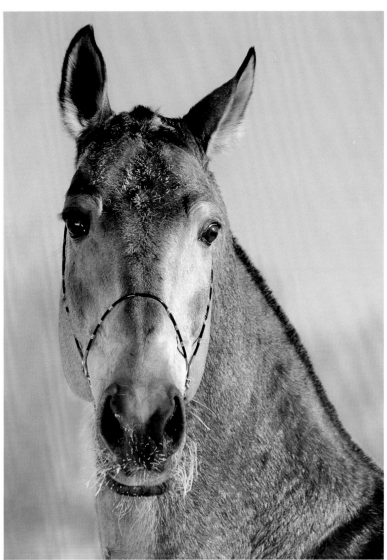

LEFT & ABOVE: The Akhal-Teke is independent, free-spirited and inclined to be willful. It requires firm, but kind and tactful handling and is unsuitable for the inexperienced. It is a proud and ancient breed, once highly prized as a warhorse.

because of their great agility and athleticism, Akhal-Tekes are most often used for racing and in endurance events.

The Akhal-Teke appears to break almost every rule of good conformation. Its head is carried high on a long, thin neck set at an angle of 45 degrees to the body, giving it a proud, slightly haughty appearance. It has a fine, elegant head with wide cheeks and a straight or slightly dished nose; the large eyes are bold and expressive. The nostrils are dry and flared and the ears shapely and alert. Although the shoulders are broad and sloping, the chest is quite narrow. The body is fairly short, rounded and shallow, and the long loins have little definition. The girth is quite narrow, and the very long legs appear disproportionately long in relation to the body, and taper to small hooves.

It has an unusually smooth-flowing and powerful action. The shape of the pasterns are unique to the breed, possibly developed from negotiating desert terrain.

The Akhal-Teke is not known for its sunny nature, in fact, quite the reverse. It is willful and rebellious and benefits from one firm handler which it can learn to trust. It is an intelligent animal which requires careful and sympathetic training; it does not respond well to punishment and may very well retaliate. Due to its genetic inheritance it is unlikely to flourish cooped up in a stable and must be allowed a predominantly outdoor life, with plenty of space to wander.

Colors may be chestnut, bay, gray, palomino, black and dun. All the colors, apart from raven black, are strikingly iridescent. Height is approximately 15.2hh, though, with its pronounced withers and high head-carriage, the horse appears taller.

ABOVE & LEFT: The Akhal-Teke has a rather unconventional conformation but the overall effect is extremely striking.

210

ARABIAN

The Arabian (Arab) is one of the oldest of the hotblooded breeds, and its bloodlines are present in many modern horses found throughout Europe and the United States. The name is not strictly accurate, as the original "Arab" may well have been a small Oriental-type wild horse, living in Eastern Europe, the Near East and the Middle East. The Arab was further developed as Islam assimilated the breed, and Muslim invaders used it as a cavalry horse. Today's modern Arabians can trace their descent from five foundation mares, known as Al-Khamesh (The Five), said to have been selected for their obedience.

The Arab was also of great importance to the Bedouin, the nomadic tribe of the desert, which can trace its association with the breed to 3000 BC, to the mare Baz and the stallion Hoshaba.

Arab horses were so-named when they were imported from the Arabian Peninsula to Britain in the 19th century. The Arab is also the foundation of the Thoroughbred. Arab blood is therefore highly effective when mixed with other breeds, and usually brings great improvements to any offspring that result.

Arabs are extremely beautiful, with a delicacy that belies their strength and stamina. They shine in riding events, such as dressage, riding horse, and in-hand showing. They also excel in disciplines that

OPPOSITE & ABOVE: Bedouin breeders carefully recorded bloodlines and jealously guarded the purity of their horses. As a result, today's Arabians are as immediately recognizable as ever.

rely on strength, such as endurance riding and racing. Arabs have the reputation of being unable to jump, which is quite untrue; they are keen jumpers, but lack the ability to compete at high level.

The head is short and refined, with a dish-shaped profile and a tapered muzzle with large nostrils. The eyes are large, wide-apart and low-set, and the ears are small, shapely and set well apart. The

THESE PAGES & OVERLEAF: The Arabian is an ancient hotblood whose bloodline has been used to improve many other breeds. It was of primary importance in the development of the Thoroughbred.

jaw is rounded and forms a curved arch where head and neck meet, known as the *mitbah*.

The back is slightly concave, with sloping shoulders and well-defined withers. The croup is level and the girth deep. The tail is set high. The legs are strong, hard and clean, with flat knees, short

THESE PAGES & OVERLEAF: Arabians, apart from their obvious beauty, are prized for their agility and stamina.

cannons, and well-defined tendons; the hooves are hard and tough. The Arab also has a distinctive skeletal feature, in that it has fewer vertebrae, i.e. 5 lumbar, 17 rib and 16 tail, compared with 6-18-18 in other breeds, giving it a short-coupled appearance.

The horse's action is as if it were floating on air. Due to their desert origins, Arabs have fine coats and skin which is designed to release heat. Consequently, they require special care in winter, though they are tougher than Thoroughbreds.

Arabs are famous for their intelligence and responsiveness. They are also affectionate and respectful of other animals, also of human beings, being especially good with children. The reverse side of their character is that they are fiery and courageous; they can also be stubborn if asked to do something against their will.

All solid colors are possible, but chestnut and gray are the most common. Arabs usually stand somewhere between 14 and 15.2hh.

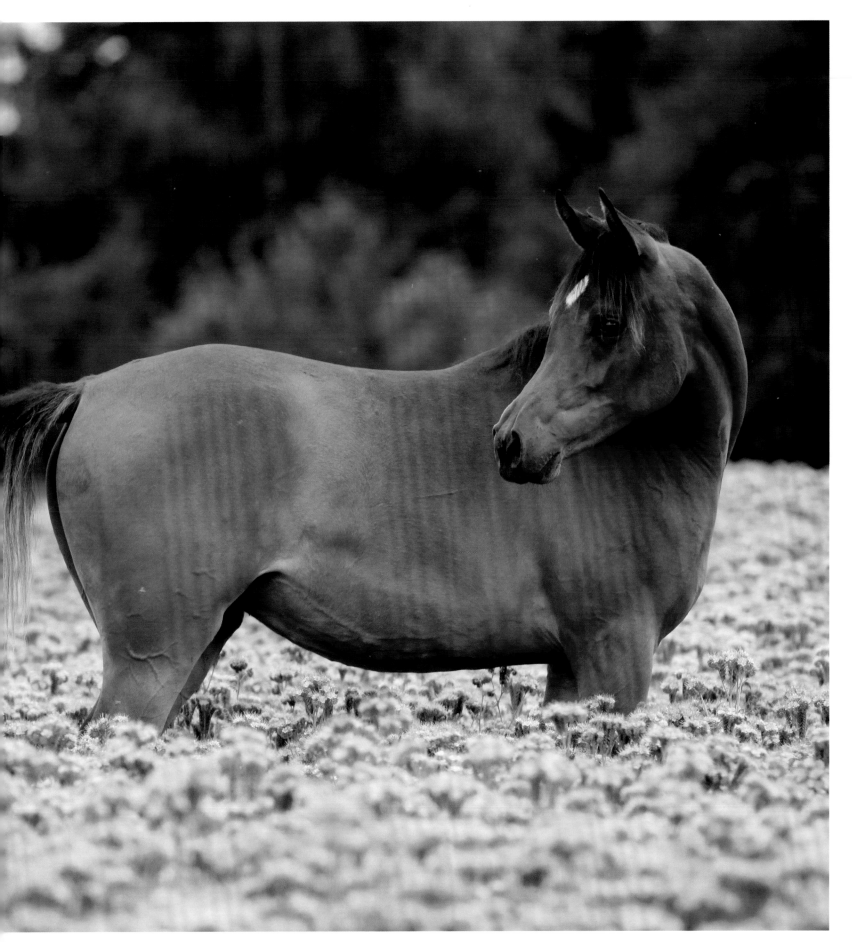

MARWARI

The Marwari, from the Marwar region of Rajasthan, is similar in appearance to the Kathiawari, but is of much greater stature; it has often been featured in Indian art over the centuries. The Marwari is unusual in that it has a fifth gait, called the *revaal*, which is a long, smooth action with little vertical movement, which makes it very comfortable to ride.

Marwari numbers declined during the British occupancy of India, but thanks to today's Rajput families, and others interested in the continuation of the breed, the Marwari is once again flourishing. It is now used as a dancing horse, popular at weddings and festivals. Its dance is a form of haute école, which the horse would have been taught when it was a warhorse long ago.

It has a high, proud head-carriage with a straight or Roman nose, its trademark ears curving inward until they almost meet in the

center. The eyes are large, bright and intelligent; the neck is of medium length and arches in movement. The coat is fine and silky.

The Marwari has a naturally flamboyant presence and loves to perform, but it is also tough and able to survive harsh conditions. It is courageous, intelligent and a willing worker.

Marwaris may be any color, including roan, piebald and skewbald. They stand between 15 and 16hh.

LEFT, ABOVE & OPPOSITE: Traditional Rajasthani literature speaks highly of the Marwari's fabulous exploits, such as its ability to leap over high city walls.

CHAPTER SIX
HORSES OF AUSTRALIA & AFRICA

*"The substitution of the internal combustion engine for the horse marked a
very gloomy milestone in the progress of mankind."*

—Sir Winston Churchill

AUSTRALIAN STOCK HORSE

The Australian Stock Horse, otherwise known as the Waler, has a history that began in the 18th century, when horses were imported into Australia from South Africa and Chile. These tended to have excellent constitutions, being descended not only from Iberian, Arab,

BELOW & RIGHT: The Waler was one of the finest cavalry horses in the world, having been used in the Indian Mutiny, the Boer Wars and First World War.

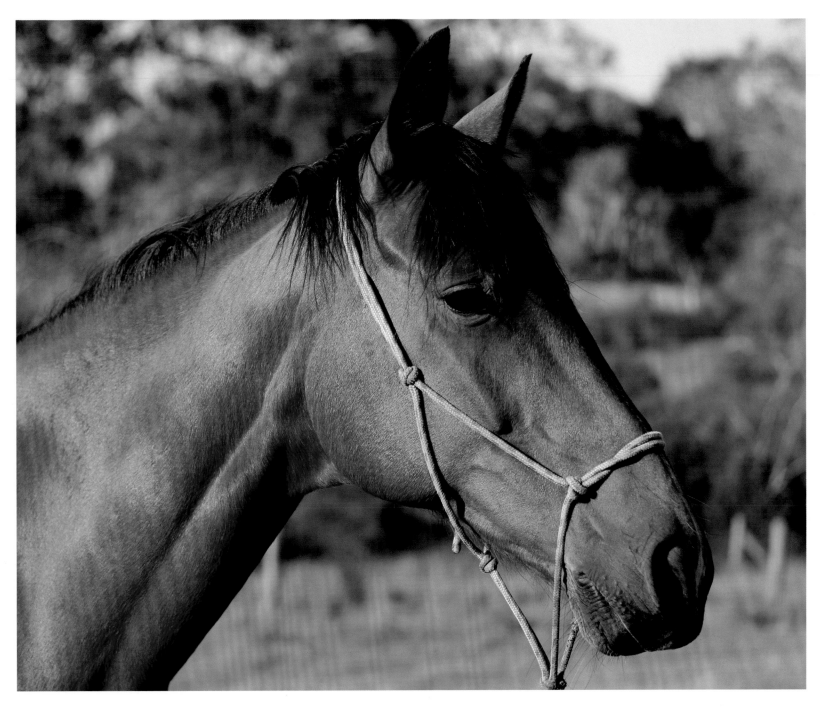

Barb, Criollo and Basuto stock, but also from Indonesian ponies. The quality of the first horses was found wanting, however, but later infusions of Arab and Thoroughbred brought great improvements to the stock.

The breed, also known as the New South Wales Horse, was once important as a cavalry horse. It was used by the British in India from about 1850, but soon became popular with stockmen, who saw its soundness and endurance as distinct assets in the huge expanses of the Australian outback; it was also used in harness.

By the 1940s, the Waler, as it was now generally known, had become a quality horse, but after the Second World War the population was allowed to dwindle. It was also bred with other horses, which subsequently weakened the breed. Today, steps are being taken to improve the Waler by adding Quarter Horse, Arab and Thoroughbred, but it has yet to be regarded as a consistent breed.

The ideal Waler has a fine head with a broad forehead, straight nose, and medium-length alert ears. The eyes are kind but inquisitive and intelligent. The neck is long and elegant with a slight crest, and the shoulders are sloping. The chest is broad with a deep girth, while the body is of medium length with strong loins and well-developed quarters. The legs are strong with shapely hooves.

The Waler has many excellent qualities. It is obedient and willing to work and is kind and intelligent. They are most often bays, though all solid colors are possible. They stand between 15 and 16.2hh.

BARB

The Barb has ancient origins, its name having been taken from a location in North Africa, once the fabled Barbary Coast, a section of the Mediterranean littoral stretching from Morocco to Egypt. Here, 2,000 years ago, cavalry horses were bred by Hannibal's Carthaginian forces.

At an early stage, the breed was probably influenced by the Arabian horse, brought to North Africa by the Arabs – also by hotblooded Oriental types. A great many were imported to Europe, particularly England, where many references to "Barbary" horses are to be found, the most famous being Richard II's "Roan Barbary." Here they were also bred for the cavalry and were prized for their speed and great stamina. Today it is difficult to find a pure-bred Barb. This is because of the widespread cross-breeding practised throughout the Mahgreb, its purpose being to produce good general riding horses.

The Barb is not a handsome horse and is inclined to be bad-tempered, but it has had a tremendous influence on other breeds, particularly in Europe and the Americas. The Andalusian of Spain, the Connemara Pony of Ireland, the Thoroughbred, and even the Criollo of South America are all believed to have Barb blood running through their veins.

Today the Barb is used for general riding, racing and display purposes. It remains very popular in its native land but receives little recognition elsewhere.

The Barb, bred for desert life, is fairly lightweight. The head is long and narrow, with a slightly dished face and medium well-shaped pointed ears; the eyes are kind and intelligent. The neck is of medium length, with a pronounced crest. The withers are prominent and the shoulders flat. The legs are fine, but strong, and the hooves are hard and well-shaped – a feature of all desert horses. The mane and tail are full, with the tail set low on flat quarters.

The Barb is quite stand-offish and inclined to be irritable, but it has a reputation for extreme toughness, speed and stamina – qualities which have made it suitable for improving other breeds.

Most common colors are black, bay and dark brown, though Barbs with Arab blood may have coats of other colors, such as gray. The height range is 14.2–15.2hh.

BELOW & OPPOSITE: The aim of the World Organization of the Barb Horse, founded in Algeria in 1987, is to preserve the breed, but it is difficult to say how its purity has been affected.

BOERPERD

The Boerperd or Boer Horse, has a history that runs side by side with the white settlers of South Africa and the arrival of the Dutch in Cape Town in 1652.

The first horses seen in the region were of Oriental blood and were imported from Java, which in turn were sold by the Dutch East India Company to the Free Burghers in 1665. Over the years, however, significant inbreeding had taken place and measures were taken to improve the breed by introducing Arabian blood to the stock.

This practice continued for 150 years until a definite type emerged, known as the Cape Horse. Meanwhile, some Iberian breeds arrived in the Cape in 1793, which may or may not have had an effect on the native horses. In the late 18th and early 19th centuries, Cape Horses remained very popular and were prized for their endurance, stamina, speed and intelligence, which made them useful in a military role.

Over the years, various other influences affected the breed, and Flemish horses, Hackneys, Norfolk Trotters and Cleveland Bays brought further improvements. The breed continued to survive, despite disease and the Boer Wars, in which the horses certainly proved their worth.

The Boerperd (Afrikaans for farm horse) owes much of its appearance to its Oriental and Arab forebears. The head is small and wedge-shaped, with a slightly dished or straight nose, and it has a small, neat muzzle with flared nostrils. The eyes are bright and intelligent and the ears are medium-sized and alert. The body is short and compact, with a neatly sloping shoulder, deep girth, and well-proportioned muscular legs with plenty of bone. The hooves are tough and shapely.

The Boerperd is spirited, courageous and intelligent, with plenty of stamina and agility. They come in most solid colors and gray, and range from 14.2–15.2hh in height.

THESE PAGES & OVERLEAF: The history of the Boer Horse runs parallel with that of the white settlers in South Africa. It took its name from the Boer Wars in which it was widely used.

CHAPTER SEVEN
HEAVY HORSES

"He knows when you're happy
He knows when you're comfortable
He knows when you're confident
And he always knows when you have carrots."
—Anonymous

BRABANT

The Brabant, or Belgian Heavy Draft Horse, comes from the area of Belgium that has Brussels as its capital. It is of ancient origin, only slightly more recent than the Ardennais, to which it owes part of its lineage: the other part of its inheritance is thought to have stemmed from the Flanders Horse of the 11th to 16th centuries, which in turn is believed to have been descended from the ancient horses of the Quaternary period. For centuries, Belgian breeders produced their stock by selective breeding, which also included inbreeding.

The Brabant's very existence is a direct result of the geology of the area: the rich heavy soil required a horse with great pulling power and big strong joints to enable it to lift its huge feet out of the thick clods of mud. As a result, three distinct bloodlines emerged 100 years ago, which intermingled to create the modern Brabant. These are the Gros

THESE PAGES & OVERLEAF: The Brabant retains its pleasing conformation despite being large. It has greatly contributed to the development of many of today's heavy breeds.

de la Dendre, which is muscular and strong with huge legs; the Gris de Nivelles, with good conformation and a certain elegance; and the Colosse de la Mehaigne, which is large and has a lively temperament.

Over the centuries, the Brabant has had an enormous influence on today's modern breeds, much in the same way as the Arab bloodline has been added to improve existing stock. In the Middle Ages the horse was imported all over Europe and its bloodlines are also present in Germany's warmbloods. The Russians introduced native breeds to it to produce working horses and its influence is also present in the Shire, Irish Draft and Clydesdale, to name but a few. Today, Brabants are still part of the foundation stock for the breeding of warmbloods. They now appear throughout the world, where they are still used in agricultural work, logging and as dray horses. They also feature in the show ring.

The head is fairly square, with a straight profile, small pricked ears, and deep-set eyes with a kindly expression. The neck is short and very strong and set high with a large crest. The shoulders are sloping and the chest is wide and deep. The body is short, with a well-muscled back and strong quarters. The legs are fairly long and muscular and the hooves are large, rounded and tough; not much feathering is present.

The Brabant is so extremely docile as to be described as almost sluggish. But it is willing and obedient, and its pulling power is equal only to that of the Shire, for which it is highly prized. It is a hard worker with plenty of stamina and a strong constitution, and requires relatively little food for its size. Brabants are usually light chestnut with a flaxen mane; also acceptable is red roan, bay, dun and gray. It is a large animal and stands somewhere between 16.1 and 17hh.

CLYDESDALE

The establishment of the Scottish Clydesdale began in the late-17th century when Lanarkshire farmers and various dukes of Hamilton supposedly imported Flemish stallions, ancestors of the Brabant, to Scotland. The farmers were skillful breeders and mated them with native heavy draft mares already in existence; over the next 100 years or so, English Shire, Friesian and Cleveland Bay blood was also added. The result was known as the Clydesdale and it was highly prized as a draft horse. The Clydesdale Horse Society was established in 1877, almost a century and a half after the breed first began to evolve.

The breed soon became popular as a general farm horse and also for hauling loads over long and short distances; Clydesdales could be found in most major cities of Scotland, the North of England and Northern Ireland, as well as in agricultural areas. In fact, the horse became popular the world over, when considerable numbers were imported to North America, Canada and Australia.

Clydesdales are very different from the usual heavy draft horses, which tend to be plain-looking and squat; in fact, it looks positively refined, having a short-coupled body, long legs, and a high head-carriage. As with all heavy horses, the Clydesdale breed began to decline with the development of motorized transport and reached an even lower ebb in the 1960s and '70s. A few families kept the breed going, however, and today numbers are rising, although the

Clydesdale continues to be classified as "at risk" by the Rare Breeds Society. Today they are highly valued in the show ring as well as in harness; as dray horses, they often take part in displays, and are even used to pull wedding carriages.

The head is proudly held, and the medium, well-shaped ears are pricked and alert; the eyes are kind and intelligent. It has a slightly Roman nose and the nostrils are large. The neck is long and well-set, with a high crest leading to high withers. The back is slightly concave and short and the quarters are well-developed and powerful. The legs are straight and long with plenty of feathering. The feet are large and require careful shoeing if contracted heels are not to develop.

These charming horses are energetic with an alert, cheerful air. They are even-tempered and enjoy company. They are extremely strong with a lively action and a slight tendency to dish.

Clydesdales can be bay, brown and black and usually have white patches all the way up the legs and under the belly, which can turn roan in places. They are usually around 16.2hh, but some males may reach 17hh or more.

THESE PAGES & OVERLEAF: The outstanding characteristics of this famous horse are a combination of weight, size and activity, but what is particularly admired is the exceptional durability of the Clydesdale's feet and limbs. It is surprisingly agile for its size.

PERCHERON

The Percheron comes from La Perche in Normandy in northern France. The breed is an ancient one, dating back to 732, when Arab horses, abandoned by the Saracens after their defeat at the Battle of Poitiers, were allowed to breed with the local heavy mares of the region. The Percheron type was the result.

At this time, the horse was much lighter than its modern counterpart and was used for riding as well as for light draft work. The type remained popular until the Middle Ages and the Crusades, when Arab and Barb horses from the Holy Land were mated with Percherons. It was also around this time that the Comte de Perche brought back Spanish horses from his forays in Spain; these were also

mated with the Percheron, with further infusions of Andalusian added at a later date.

By the 18th century, the original breed had become almost completely eradicated by additions of Thoroughbred and more Arab; in 1820 two gray Arab stallions were mated with Percheron mares, thus creating the predominantly gray color of the modern-day breed.

By now all the heaviness of the ancient breed had disappeared; consequently, heavy mares from other regions were bred with Percheron stallions to make them more suitable for agriculture and to formulate the breed as it is known today. The lighter Percheron still exists and is used as a heavy riding horse, while the heavy version is still used for farm and forestry work and, in some countries, for pulling drays. It is also popular in the show ring.

LEFT, ABOVE & OPPOSITE BOTH: The Percheron has had a large part to play in France's long history. There are two types of Percheron: the light version is used as a riding horse, while its heavier counterpart is still used on farms and for forestry work.

Over the years the Percheron has been heavily exported to other countries, such as the U.K., Canada, Australia and other parts of Europe, which has helped in its recognization as one of the world's leading heavy breeds.

The Percheron's head is proud and elegant, for a heavy breed, with a straight nose, broad forehead, expressive eyes, and short, shapely ears. The neck is short to medium, well-developed and with great strength. The shoulders are nicely sloping and well-shaped, with a broad chest and a deep girth. The Percheron is fairly short in the back, which adds to its strength, with slightly sloping but broad quarters. The legs are short and sturdy, with well-shaped tough hooves with very little feather.

The Percheron possesses a good deal of elegance due to the large amounts of Arab blood that have been added over the centuries. It has an excellent temperament, is calm, obedient and easy to handle, and has a keen intelligence. It has a smooth but lively action which makes it comfortable to ride.

Mainly gray, Percherons can occasionally be black or dark chestnut. There are two types: the small Percheron, which stands between 14.1 and 16.1hh, and the large, which is somewhere between 16.1 and 17.3hh.

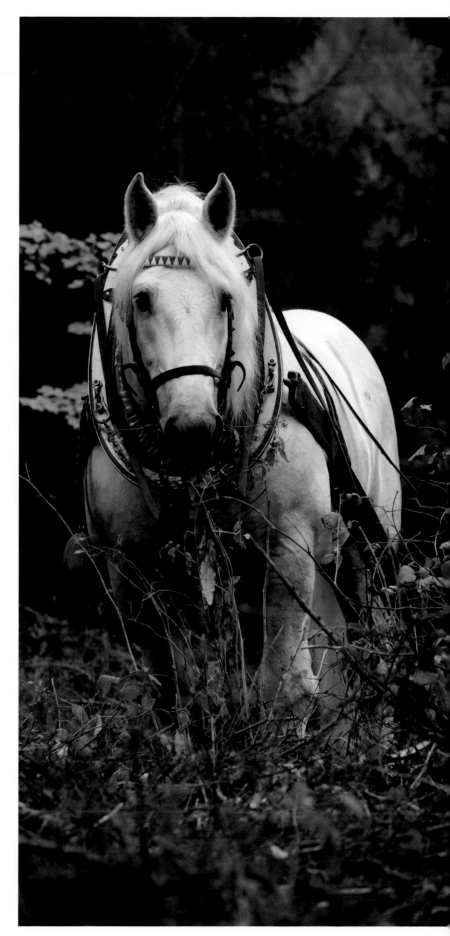

SHIRE

The English Shire is one of the most famous and distinctive of all the draft horses and one of the largest and most majestic breeds in the world. Descended from medieval warhorses, whose immense strength enabled them to carry knights into battle wearing full armor, it was probably based on the Friesian horse, with later infusions of Brabant. It was brought to England by the Dutch to drain the fens of East Anglia, but it was not until the late 19th century that the best heavy horses in England were selected to develop the breed as it is known today.

The Shire's strength also made it suitable for agriculture and heavy haulage work, so initially the breed was established in Lincolnshire and Cambridgeshire, where strong horses were required to cope with heavy fenland soil; but the Shire soon became widespread in Staffordshire, Leicestershire and Derbyshire, until it eventually spread over England as a whole.

Up until the 1930s, the Shire was widely seen across the country, but numbers dropped dramatically when mechanization of farming began to appear, putting the breed in danger of disappearing

BELOW & OPPOSITE: With an enormous capacity for weight-pulling, Shires have held the world records for both largest overall horse and tallest horse at various times in the past.

altogether. Fortunately, the problem was detected by a few dedicated breeders, who helped to promote the breed and restore it to its former glory.

The Shire Horse Society has worked tirelessly to raise funds and encourage the spread of the breed to other countries. Today, there are active Shire Horse societies across Europe, the United States, Canada and Australia. Although a few Shires are still used on farms today, they are kept mainly for the sheer pleasure of working them in their traditional roles. They are also used in plowing competitions, again, for pleasure, and for the same reason are used in pairs by breweries to deliver beer locally; the spectacle obviously makes for excellent publicity.

The Shire's most significant feature is its sheer size and massive muscular conformation. It is the largest and strongest horse in the world and weighs a ton or more when mature. Built ultimately for strength, the chest is wide, the back short-coupled, the loins and quarters massive. The legs, joints and feet are sufficiently large to balance and support the Shire's weight; the lower legs are covered with long, straight, silky feathers. In the show ring, white feathers are generally preferred as they help to accentuate the horse's action.

Even though the Shire is such a large horse, it is not an ungainly heavyweight; in fact it is very much in proportion and quite awesome to behold. The head is always noble, the nose slightly Roman, and the eyes are large and wise.

The Shire is well-known for its patient, gentle and placid nature; it is a true "gentle giant." In fact, it is quite amazing that such a strong animal weighing so much can be so easily handled, and it is not uncommon to see them ridden or handled by children or small women. Its kindness is legendary.

Black, brown and gray are the recognized colors of the breed. White feathers on the legs are preferred for the show ring, and white face markings are common. They stand somewhere between 16.2 and 18hh.

THESE PAGES & OVERLEAF: The Shire is the largest and strongest horse in the world; it is also the most elegant and majestic of the heavy horses.

SUFFOLK PUNCH

The Suffolk Horse, usually known as the Suffolk Punch, originated in East Anglia in England. It takes its name from the county of Suffolk, while "punch" is an old word meaning "short and thickset." It is thought to date back to 1506 and is the oldest heavy breed in Britain.

The breed was first developed by crossing the native heavy mares of the region with imported French Norman stallions. Modern-day Suffolks, however, can be traced back on the male side to a single, nameless stallion, foaled in 1768 and belonging to Thomas Crisp of Orford, near Woodbridge, Suffolk. Even though the breed is relatively pure, infusions of Norfolk Trotter, Thoroughbred and Cob were added during the centuries that followed.

Immensely strong, it is also quite agile, due to its relatively small size. These qualities, combined with a lack of feather on the legs, like

BELOW & OPPOSITE: While the great warhorses of medieval times were still locked in mortal combat on the battlefield, East Anglian farmers were quietly developing their very own breed of heavy horse: the Suffolk Punch.

the Percheron, made it ideal for working the heavy clay soils of East Anglia. Moreover, its economical food consumption, in proportion to its size, enabled it to work for long days on the farm without stopping.

As with many of the heavy breeds, numbers fell dangerously low when farm tractors became widespread. Today, Suffolks are rare, even though there has been a concerted effort to increase numbers in recent years. Today, Suffolks are shown, used in plowing competitions, or are kept by breweries for their novelty value.

The Suffolk Punch is always chestnut in color (the traditional spelling in this instance is chesnut, without the "t"). The breed is well-known for its great strength, and its extremely powerful, muscular

body, with relatively short legs, provides a low center of gravity; this enables the horse to pull plows or vehicles that much more easily. Suffolks mature early and can do light work when they are 2 years old. They continue working well into their 20s.

The Suffolk is docile and hardworking. It is capable of almost any kind of work and is easy to maintain. Height is between 16.1 and 17.1hh.

BELOW & OPPOSITE: The Suffolk Punch is Britain's oldest breed, dating back to 1506. Sadly, they are now quite rare.

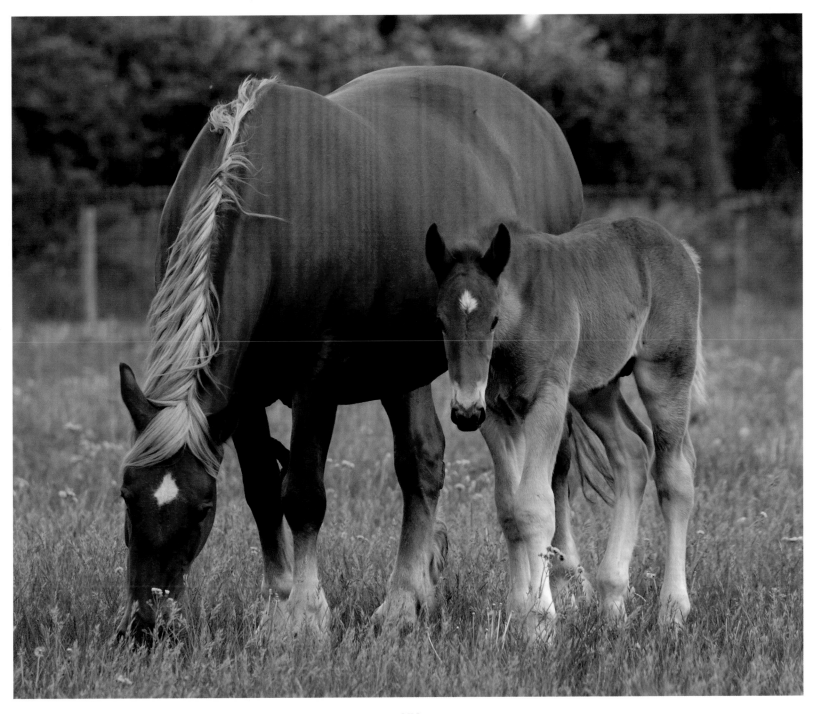

INDEX

A

Akhal-Teke 206–211
Altér Real 53, 76–77, 83
American Miniature 32–35
American Saddlebred 36–39, 54, 74
American Shetland 40–41
American Warmblood 169
Andalusian 53, 65, 78–85, 109, 128, 136, 140, 142, 145, 180, 226, 242
Anglo-Arab 14, 86–87, 202
Anglo-Norman 106, 136, 152
Appaloosa 24, 42–47, 50, 66, 139
Arab (Arabian) 14, 18, 22, 40, 42, 48, 50, 54, 66, 78, 86, 87, 90,113, 118, 120, 126, 140, 152, 164, 177, 180, 186, 191, 194, 196,198, 200, 202, 212–221, 225, 226, 230, 242
Ardennais 234
Asiatic Wild Horse (see Przewalski's Horse)
Australian Stock Horse 224–225

B

Barb 22, 53, 64, 65, 78, 126, 136, 140, 180, 225, 226–227, 242
Bashkir Curly 184–185
Basuto (Basotho) Pony 225, 228–229
Belgian Heavy Draft (see Brabant)
Belgian Warmblood 169, 170
Boerperd (Boer Horse) 230–233
Brabant 234–237, 238
Brandenburg 124
British Warmblood 169
Brumby 9, 10–13
Byerley Turk 161

C

Camargue 14–17
Cape Horse 228, 230
Carthusian 83
Cayuse Indian Pony 24
Celtic Pony 98, 102, 126, 132, 148, 155, 174

Chickasaw Indian Pony 24
Cleveland Bay 83, 124, 130, 152, 166, 230, 238
Clydesdale 89, 115, 126, 237, 238–241
Connemara 88–89, 132, 226
Criollo 53, 225, 226

D

Dales Pony 98, 109, 115, 149
Danish Warmblood 169, 194
Darley Arabian 161
Dartmoor 90–93, 94, 149
Døle 132
Don 186–189
Drummer Horse (see Gypsy Vanner)
Dutch Harddraver 194
Dutch Warmblood 169, 171–173

E

Eclipse 161
English Shire 115, 166, 237, 238, 244–249
Eurasian Wild Horse (see Tarpan)
Exmoor 94–97, 149

F

Falabella 48–51
Fell 98–101, 109, 149
Fjord 102–105, 132
Flanders Horse 234
Florida Cracker Horse (Chickasaw Indian Pony) 24
French Anglo-Arab 86
French Trotter 106–107
Friesian 101, 108–111, 115, 152, 238
Furioso 112–113

G

Galloway 126
Garrano 145
Gidrán 86
Godolphin Arabian 161
Gypsy Vanner 114–117

H

Hackney 40, 89, 106, 180, 230
Haflinger 118–121
Hanoverian 122–125, 136, 152, 169
Herod 161
Highland 126–127, 132, 149
Hispano-Arab 86
Holstein 128–131, 169
Hungarian Anglo-Arab (see Gidrán)

I

Icelandic 132–135
Irish Cob 115
Irish Draft 89, 237

K

Kabardin 190–193
Karabakh 186
Kathiawari 222
Kladruber 136–137, 140
Knabstrup 138–139
Konik 18–21

L

Lipizzaner 83, 136, 140–143
Lusitano 76, 77, 83, 142, 144–147

M

Mangalarga Marchador 52–53
Marsh Horse 128
Marwari 222–223
Matchem 161
Mecklenburg 122, 124, 194
Missouri Fox Trotter 54–55
Mongolian (see Przewalski's Horse)
Morgan 38, 54, 56–57, 72, 74
Mustang 9, 22–27

N

Narragansett Pacer 36, 74
Neapolitan 128, 136, 140
New Forest Pony 148–151

New South Wales (see Australian Stock Horse)
Nonius 113
Norfolk Roadster 90, 106, 113
Norfolk Trotter 230
Norman 106
North Star. (see Furioso)

O

Old Don (see Don)
Oldenburg 136, 152–153
Orlov (Orloff) Trotter 106, 109, 186, 194–197, 202

P

Paint Horse (see Pinto)
Park Morgan (see Morgan)
Paso Fino 64, 62–63, 65
Percheron 126, 242–243, 253
Peruvian Paso 62, 64–65
Peruvian Stepping Horse (see Peruvian Paso)
Pinto 58–61
Plantation Horse (see Tennessee Walking Horse)
Pleasure Morgan (see Morgan)
Pony of the Americas 66–67
Postier Breton 14
Powys Cob (Powys Rouncy) see Welsh Cob
Przewalski's Horse 9, 28–31, 102

Q

Quarter Horse 42, 66, 68–71, 225

S

Selle Français 106, 169
Shagya Arabian 86, 198–201
Shetland 40, 48, 50, 66, 132, 154–157
Shire (see English Shire)
Sorraia Pony 78, 145
Standardbred 38, 72–73, 74, 106, 196
Strelets-Arab 86, 202
Suffolk Punch 250–253

T

Tarpan 9, 18, 20, 102, 191
Tennessee Walking Horse 54, 74–75
Tersky (Tersk) 202–205
Thoroughbred 14, 38, 40, 48, 50, 54, 56, 66, 72, 74, 86, 87, 89, 90, 106, 113, 124, 130, 139, 152, 158–161, 163, 164, 186, 191, 194, 202, 213, 225, 226, 228, 242
Trakehner 124, 152, 162–165, 202
Turkmene (Turkoman) 186, 191, 206

W

Waler (see Australian Stock Horse)
Warmblood 166–173
Welsh Cob 56, 83, 89, 90, 174, 180
Welsh Mountain Pony 174, 177, 179, 180
Welsh Pony 90, 149, 174, 179, 180
Welsh Pony of Cob Type 174, 179, 180
Westphalian 124, 152, 182–183

Y

Yorkshire Coach Horse 130, 152, 180